Contents

The Basic Principles:
A Guide to Federal Benefits and Financial Planning

Federal Edition

RICK GARNITZ

LifeSpan Services, Inc.
Decatur, Georgia

Another product in

Copyright ©2012 by LifeSpan Services, Inc. All Rights Reserved. No part of this book covered by the copyright hereon may be reproduced or copied in any form or by any means — graphic, electronic, or mechanical, including photocopying, taping, or information storage and retrieval systems without written permission of the publisher.

ISBN 0-927289-94-6

Printed in the United States of America

LifeSpan Services, Inc.
235 East Ponce de Leon Avenue
Decatur, Georgia 30030

404-373-2548

www.lifespan-services.com
info@lifespan-services.com

Abraham Lincoln said, "You can't escape the responsibility of tomorrow by evading it today." That simple statement is even more important to keep in mind today . . . as uncertain economic times confront us. The Basic Principles is your guide to taking responsibility for building the kind of future you've always envisioned. The earlier you begin to plan, the better off you will be.

In our thirties and forties, our work, our families, and our finances are the issues we worry about most. This guide addresses planning in each of these areas.

You'll need to understand your retirement benefits and how to maximize the advantages of the tax deferred savings plans. Retiring workers often discover too late that, if they had only made a few mid-career adjustments in their planning, they could have avoided a pre-retirement scramble.

We hope this guide gives you the skills you need to plan the best years of your life. All the best for the years ahead!

Rick Garnitz

First Things First

Credit card debt is sinking me! How can I get out of debt?
Should I concentrate on tax-deferred savings or paying down debt?
How do I deal with a spender when I'm a saver?
Why do I need to monitor my income and out-go?

The way you manage your money determines how much money you will have not only for tomorrow but for next year, five years from now, and for a lifetime. Remember, you control your financial destiny. You are responsible for what you earn and what you spend. Cash planning is essential in preparing for your future and the future of your family.

Controlling Debt

Cash planning is taking control of debt. **Controlling debt is the single most important money management action you can take.** This chapter explores the basic principles of cash planning to help you control your debt. These principles include distinguishing your wants from your needs, setting goals, paying down credit card debt, and budgeting.

Many people need a shove before they do serious cash planning. What motivates you? Do you fear a future of financial need? Do you envision a future in which you are comfortable, secure, and free from the need to worry or work? Regardless of your specific situation or goals, the earlier you begin systematic planning, the better off you'll be.

You should understand cash planning before you move into financial planning and investing. Cash planning teaches debt control and if you don't control debt, it won't matter how much you understand or learn about investing. Without debt control, any financial planning you do will be of little use. Once you have learned to control debt, your financial planning and investing will be easier and you will be more successful. Most importantly, when you have learned to make planning a habit, all areas of life will be less stressful.

Wants versus Needs

The first step in successful cash planning is to differentiate between your wants and your needs, and develop a strategy to deal with each. Everyone has wants and everyone has needs, and sometimes it is difficult to distinguish between them. One guideline: wants can be postponed; needs cannot. You should pay attention to needs first. Postpone achieving your wants until after you have attained your needs, or at least set in motion the means of attaining them. The most important element is not sacrifice, but understanding your needs. This may require delaying certain wants, but your reward will be in knowing that your future will be more secure.

Money Talk

How we manage, barely manage, or mismanage our finances becomes more complex when decisions must be made by two people instead of one. Making joint decisions requires communication. It requires talking about money. Discussions about spending, saving, prioritizing, and allocating money enter areas filled with emotional, philosophical, and psychological land mines. Say the wrong thing, use the wrong tone of voice, grin when you should look serious, and talks about money can blow up in your face.

You think saving for your son's education should come before lending your brother-in-law more money. Your partner feels that present-day family needs take precedence over future needs. You think a newer car is an urgent need; he thinks the roof on the house is more pressing. We learn early in life how to talk, or not talk, about money. We listened as our parents cussed, discussed, or refused to communicate. Some of us heard that money matters were adult issues; and as children, we were not involved.

Few of us have been taught how to negotiate financial flash points. What we learned as children — good or bad — we bring to our adult discussions and money management practices. Some of us reason and plead; others manipulate and demand. We open with trusting communication and often end up negotiating in bitterness and anger. So what is the answer? Is there an answer? Yes and no. It depends on your ability to embrace change. You must know yourself, your values and priorities. This provides the basis from which you can communicate your genuine feelings. The issue is rarely simply money. The real question is what is most important to you, and to your partner. How well are you communicating what is important to you and how well do you understand what is important to your partner? How much are you willing to give, or take, on any single issue? Unless your relationship is a high priority, unless you are willing to entertain the idea of a compromise, your discussions will end up being arguments without an end and neither of you will be happy.

The answer lies in understanding yourself and each other, in communicating your values clearly and openly welcoming a win/win solution. Neither of you may get exactly or all of what you want, but the joint decision can represent the best possible accommodation between the two views. And don't overlook the by-products of the process — peace in the household, less arguing, achieving common goals, and joint successes.

Setting Goals

Turn your needs into goals by writing them down and ranking them. Establishing your objectives and priorities is critically important. Goals can be short-term — new carpeting for the den; or long-term — a home, college education, or retirement income. Whatever your goals, your first priority should be an emergency fund equal to three to six months of your take-home pay.

What financial goals are you working toward? Estimate the cost of your goals and set a date for their completion. Write your goals in three intervals.

Interval	Goal	Estimated Cost	Estimated Date
Six Months	Emergency fund (3-6 months pay)		
One Year			
Five Years			

Keep goals as specific as possible. One goal may be financing your child's education. Rather than saying, "Set aside some money each month for college," say, "Deposit $250 dollars each month in a 529 college savings account until I have $30,000." This states the goal in a way that will help you determine when it has been successfully reached. Some long-term goals may have to be broken into segments, with one segment worked on at a time.

Credit Card Debt

Don't think about saving or investing until you have debt under control. Debt is pervasive; many of us struggle to live within our means. Controlling debt has to be learned, and it must be practiced daily. Take the time necessary to understand the importance of debt control. Discuss these issues with your spouse or planning partner and, most importantly, learn to eliminate (or at least limit) debt.

Cut Up Your Cards. If reducing debt involves cutting up your credit cards, do it! Paying off your credit card balances will pay off with substantial savings. For example, if you're paying 18 percent interest on a credit card balance, and your average balance is $1,000, you pay $180 per year in interest charges. If you pay off that debt, the effect is the same as getting $180 per year in extra income, tax free. A person in the 28 percent tax bracket would have to earn $250 per year on a $1,000 investment (or 25 percent!) to have $180 after taxes. In turbulent times, very few investments return 25 percent. Most investments don't return 10.9 percent, 12.9 percent, or 16.9 percent, which is what typical credit cards charge. Since consumer interest charges are not tax deductible, the interest you pay monthly on each card, wisely invested, could be working for you rather than against you.

In 2012, the average U.S. interest rate on revolving credit card accounts was 14 percent. The average balance maintained was $10,678 according to CardWeb.com, a research firm. That is up 29 percent from 2000. Over the last 30 years, credit has become available to almost everyone and paying on credit has become a way of life for Americans. It was not always like that.

Consumer spending accounted for 70 percent of what has driven our national economy (GDP). Living within one's means became difficult when we had the narcotic of so much easy credit. That is ending! Consumer spending has contracted in response to the deep recession.

Get Help. If taking control of credit card debt involves getting assistance, contact the local Consumer Credit Counseling Service office. This nonprofit organization can help you contact creditors, work out repayment plans, and get you back on your feet.

Have a Heart-to-Heart. If reducing debt involves a heart-to-heart with a spouse or teenager, do it! If you are a saver and your partner is a spender, you may have to invent creative solutions so you both agree on how much to spend and where to spend it. Saving is a habit; so is spending. You can control or break old habits and you can learn new ones. You must deal with the situation together. Keep discussions going until you can agree on budgets, expenses, and strategies. With encouragement and support, a spender can become a saver — or at least spend with more self-control.

Don't Abuse Your Credit. The Consumer Credit Counseling Service cautions: If you don't think of credit as a form of debt, then you may be experiencing a warning sign of credit abuse.

Here are other warning signs of credit abuse:

- Using credit cards impulsively
- Charging to the limit on credit cards
- Paying the minimum amount due each month
- Taking out a consolidation loan to pay off credit card balances
- Using cash advances on one credit card to pay off another or other bills.

Climb Out of the Credit Card Hole. Many people are hurt by the ease of obtaining credit and the long time required to pay it off and become debt free. Like alcoholism, excessive spending is an addiction, and recovery begins with the awareness that you have a problem. Use every weapon in your arsenal to win the war on debt. If you're in over your head, here are some strategies to help you.

1. Pay down your highest debt first. Your largest debt takes the biggest bite out of your paycheck, especially if the interest rate on that debt is more than 15 percent. If you have money in savings or investments, and you cannot get a rate of return within 3 percentage points of the interest charged on the debt, pull the savings/investment immediately to pay down your debt.

   If you are currently funding a tax-deferred savings plan but your debt is excessive, reduce your contributions by 50 percent and put the rest into immediate debt reduction. If this still is not reducing large debts fast enough, suspend tax-deferred contributions and take care of the debts first.

2. If your debt seems insurmountable, break it into smaller chunks. Set a goal to pay off the first $500 or $1,000, and then tackle the next amount.

3. Reduce expenses to free up funds to pay debts. Take your lunch to work; don't buy new clothes; drive your paid-off car until you are debt-free.

4. Do consider switching to a cheaper card, but keep in mind that a lower interest rate won't solve your problem. Your goal is to be debt-free. If your current card charges 18 percent, you could save $450 on an average balance of $5,000 by switching to a card with a rate of 9 percent.

5. Don't use a card you're trying to pay off. A good strategy is to cut up the card so the debt won't increase. If you must use the card, pay off the new charges in addition to the amount you budgeted as a monthly goal.

6. Make a commitment to put any extra funds toward debt reduction. Tax refunds, cash gifts, and garage sale profits can amount to a hefty sum in a year. Don't consider such sums "found" money. Maximize their value by reducing the debt that is draining your budget.

7. Consider, but be wary of, refinancing debt using a home equity loan. Be aware that a home equity loan puts your house at risk. If you choose this route, you're consolidating all debt by borrowing on the equity in your house at, typically, a lower interest rate than most credit cards charge.

8. If you're in over your head, get help. Contact creditors on your own. Let them know you're creditworthy and want to work out a payment plan. Contact the local office of the Consumer Credit Counseling Service.

9. Don't give up. Old habits die hard! If you miss your goal the first month, ask yourself what went wrong. Are you spending on impulse or buying items not in your budget? Keep trying. Remember, once the debt is paid, you'll be able to increase your savings.

Managing Your Money

The principles of cash planning today are not that different from those of your grandparents. The fundamentals are the same — don't allow your expenses to exceed your income, and save for a rainy day. However, money management today is more difficult due to the many options and credit plans offered to consumers. How is your cash planning health?

Take the following test to find out. Select one answer for each question.

The "Broke" Test

1. How much money do you have in savings?

Two weeks take-home pay	0
Three months take-home pay	1
Six months take-home pay	2

2. What fraction of your take-home pay do you save?

None to 2 percent	0
3 to 6 percent	1
7 percent or more	2

3. How much of your credit card purchases do you pay off each month?

The entire balance	2
The balance, most of the time	1
The minimum payment	0

4. How much of your take-home pay is spent for credit payments?

5 percent or less	2
10 to 20 percent	1
More than 20 percent	0

5. What is your maximum medical insurance coverage?

$5,000 or less (or have none)	0
$5,000 to $25,000	1
More than $25,000	2

6. How often do you pay bills by the due date, not the late payment date?

Always	2
Sometimes	1
Never	0

7. What % of your take-home pay is spent for housing and utilities?

50 percent or more	0
Between 25 and 50 percent	1
Less than 25 percent	2

8. How many times a year do you use your savings to pay bills?

Six times	0
Three times	1
None	2

9. In addition to a savings program, your investments are:

Conservative (savings accounts, CDs only)	1
Mixed (savings, stocks, real estate)	2
I have none	0

10. What percentage of your current income will your retirement plan provide (including Social Security)?

60 percent or more, with inflation protection	2
Less than 60 percent, with inflation protection	1
Less than 60 percent, no inflation protection	0

Add up your points. Your total score shows the condition of your cash planning health. Any question with a score of 0 is an issue that needs your attention.

0 - 9 = Critical   10 - 14 = Fair   15 - 20 = Good

Dual-Income Planning

Cash planning can be complicated by the shifting roles between partners. Today most couples, whether they have one income or two, try to share responsibilities. No single money management system is right for everyone. Individual needs, interests, skills, attitudes and even personalities must be considered. Here are some suggestions.

- Set up a filing system for cancelled checks, bills and receipts. Such records are essential for preparing income tax returns and for resolving any disputes with stores, credit card companies, and banks.
- Keep important financial papers, including insurance policies, mortgage agreements, and old tax returns, in one place known to both partners.
- Maintain a savings as well as a checking account. If you find it difficult to save, consider joining an automatic payroll deduction plan where you work. Couples with young children should save at least 5 percent of their income, increasing this to 20 percent when children are grown. This isn't money taken away from you; it's money you put away for yourself.

- Pay all credit card balances by the due date to avoid finance charges.
- Discuss all major purchases in advance with your spouse. Be sure you both agr: e on what is a major expense.

In many two-income households, the partners agree on a formula for their respective contributions to basic living expenses. Some couples divide the bills; each paying certain bills from their salary. Such a formula works well as long as both partners agree that it's fair, and each has some money left over to meet personal needs.

Pay Yourself First

Get in the habit of saving. When you pay bills, pay yourself first. Saving regularly is the best thing you can do for your financial future. Set aside some money for savings, even a small amount, before paying other expenses. Try to save 10 percent of your gross income; but start with much less if you haven't been saving at all. Decide how much you can save, and record this amount as a fixed expense. Trying to save by putting aside whatever money is left over after bills are paid usually results in saving little, if anything.

It is important to make saving a habit, no matter how much or how little you can save. Interest earned today ensures security for tomorrow. Letting interest compound can, over time, turn modest savings into substantial amounts. The sooner you begin, the more interest you will earn. No one can afford *not* to take advantage of payroll deduction, the Thrift Savings Plan, 401ks, profit-sharing plans. Your contributions are automatically deducted. Tax-deferred savings plans offer not only tax advantages, but also provisions under which your employer matches a percentage of your contribution.

Lending Money

If a friend or a family member asks for a loan, what do you do? Saying no is never easy, but the alternative can range from a simple misunderstanding to a full-blown crisis. Making a loan always carries risk. Try to minimize the risk by making the loan as business-like as possible. State in writing the loan amount, payment amount, interest rate (if any), and any late-payment provisions, and have both parties sign and date the document.

If your adult child asks you for money, and you want to help, you might consider making the loan as an advance against their inheritance or give it as a gift. There is always the chance, however, of sibling resentment, whether or not they need money. Try to avoid family problems by openly discussing the loan (gift). Just as in investing your money, only you can decide whether and how much you can loan to a friend or family member.

Creating a Plan

As you create your plan, discuss it with your spouse or planning partner. For couples planning together, agreeing on goals, priorities, and achievement strategies is of enormous importance. Keep your communication open; keep your list short and achievable with effort. Set reasonable and measurable objectives so you can successfully implement your plan. Update your goals and strategies as your needs or finances change.

Budgeting Basics

Some people use budgets all the time. Others work on the theory that "I know how much I make and about how much I spend." Your expenses are important, whether you budget in a formal, written sense or guesstimate. Budgeting does not evoke a lot of enthusiasm, yet it is essential to successful money management. Your budget is simply your spending plan. You have one whether or not you write it down, discuss it, or think about it. A written plan helps, not hinders, you to reach your goals. The time you invest now will save time and pay off in real dollars. Your plan is the one best suited to your income, needs, and family. You can't adopt someone else's plan; your plan is the only one that will work for you.

What are your weekly cash expenditures? Do you know? A good way to find out is to carry a note pad and list expenses daily. Don't forget about the cup of coffee you buy on the way to work or the weekly stop at the doughnut shop. List everything and then analyze your list. It may be tedious, but you will get a clear idea of where your money is going.

What are your monthly expenses? You can find out by looking at your cancelled checks or online banking records and receipts from one month. Most of these amounts (mortgage, utilities, car payments, charge accounts) probably represent monthly payments. What are your projected expenses?

Use your monthly expenses as a basis for estimating your future expenses. It may help to look at the bills you can average over time. For instance, you may have your utilities averaged over a full year so you're paying the same amount every month.

Do you have control over the way you spend your money? Successful money managers control their spending; they use their money to accomplish the things that are important to them. They manage their money instead of letting it manage them. Living within your means requires planning, self-discipline, and the ability to say no to unnecessary spending. Cash planning professionals suggest the following guidelines for all spending. Expenses are grouped into five categories: housing, savings, transportation, debt, and all other expenses.

- Don't spend more than 30 percent of your net income on rent or mortgage, utilities, insurance, taxes, and home maintenance.
- Save 10 – 15 percent of your income throughout your working life.
- Limit transportation costs to 20 percent of your net income including car payments, insurance, tag or license, maintenance, gasoline, and parking.
- Keep all debt to 15 percent, including student loans, retail installment contracts, credit card purchases, personal loans, and taxes.
- All other expenses (food, child care, clothing, medical expenses, contributions, and entertainment, etc.) should not exceed 20 percent.

Balancing Income and Expenses

A successful money management plan has three basic steps:
- Estimating income and assets
- Estimating expenses
- Balancing income and expenses

Step 1: List your income and estimate other assets on the work sheet on the next page. When recording income, use your take-home pay not your gross income. Use current sources and try not to omit any information.

Income & Assets   Ownership

	#1	#2	Single	Joint
Take-home Salary				
Commission/Bonus				
Pension				
Savings Accounts				
Employer Savings Plan, etc.				
401k/TSP/403b, etc.				
Mutual Funds				
Treasuries: Notes, Bills, Bonds				
CDs				
Stocks				
Bonds				
Part-time Job				
Alimony/Child support				
Unemployment Compensation				
Real Estate/Rental Income				
Other Income				
Total Income				

Step 2: Determine how much you are spending and what you are spending it on. Consult your records to make accurate estimates. If your records are inadequate, spend time collecting the information.

Estimating Expenses	*Current*		*Projected*	
	Month	*Year*	*Add 3%*	*Next Yr*
Housing: Mortgage or Rent				
Utilities/Maintenance				
Food				
Clothing/Personal Care				
Transportation				
Car Payments				
Car Expenses				
Medical/Drugs				
Doctors/Dentists				
Income Tax				
Property Tax				
Life Insurance				
Health Insurance				
Automobile Expenses				
Property Expenses				
Entertainment				
Travel/Recreation				
Debt/Loans				
Charge Accounts				
Contributions				
Family Support				

Estimating Expenses	Current		Projected	
	Month	**Year**	**Add 3%**	**Next Yr**
Education				
Child Care				
Savings				
Miscellaneous				
Total Expenses				

Step 3: When you have completed both charts, compare your total income with your total expenses. If your income covers your expenses, meets your goals and you are satisfied with the results, you are finished (and lucky). If your expenses amount to more than your income, you have a balancing act to begin. Reevaluate all parts of your plan. Look at your flexible expenses first. See where they might be reduced, where you might be spending more than necessary. Try other strategies to control expenses.

If reducing expenses doesn't bring your expenditures in line with your available income, you may want to think about ways of increasing your income. Consider further education, on-the-job or cross-training to enhance your marketability. In extreme cases, a part-time second job may be an answer. If you are married, and either you or your spouse is not currently working, you might consider becoming a dual-income family. You may have to revise goals, rearrange priorities, and delay some expenditures. Estimate the resources needed to accomplish these goals. Resources needed may be money required, time needed, advice sought, family consulted, or anything else that serves as a stepping stone to success. Putting this all down on paper, developing a strategy and sticking with it, dramatically increases your chances of successfully achieving your goals.

This due diligence is a tool for getting what you want by living within your means. Use it as a way to make financial self-sufficiency easier. We aren't advocating that you become a slave to your budget. A balancing act is required. You must balance your commitment to budgeting and your family/personal needs. The need for balance is intuitive but there will be cases where legitimate needs will occasionally present problems. Each of these detours in your long-range budgeting and goal-setting needs to be carefully thought through. When you do have a budgeting issue, keep in mind that life and budgets are always a series of decisions that require balancing. What is important is keeping your long-range goals and the means to achieve them in focus and on track.

CHAPTER 2

Challenging Financial Times

I've done minimal financial planning. How do I start?
I'm fully funding my tax-deferred savings plan. What else do I need to do?
What are the most common financial planning mistakes?
How do I save for my young child's college education?

The stock market and world economies have had a bumpy ride. We all wonder when markets will become more consistent, when the "right" decision will become clear. Markets are never truly consistent for long periods. New legislation will affect how you save and manage your money. In 2013, a changing Social Security system may impact your potential retirement income. You can make sense of the chaos. Wise investors stay informed of such changes. With careful planning, everyone can use change to our advantage.

In this environment, planning cautiously and continually will help decrease your anxiety and increase your security . . . both financial security and, more important, emotional security. None of this is easy, but all of it is necessary. Begin with cash planning, then build your understanding of financial planning, and finally learn how to ease into the risks of investing. Begin by learning, then practicing, the basics. When you are comfortable take the next step. A good starting point is assessing where you are now and what your future needs might be. We'll cover common stumbling blocks, savings options, inflation, and college funding strategies. Let's get started.

How Well Prepared Are You?

Assess your current financial condition, estimate your future needs, and develop a plan. Build in the flexibility to change as your needs or goals change. Your first step to successful planning should be to control or eliminate debt. Once that is accomplished, you can focus on ways to protect your money and make it grow. Protecting money means holding on to what you have. True protection means maintaining your money's purchasing power.

Assessing Your Current Condition

The following questions will help you assess how financially prepared you are. They are designed to identify planning areas that may need more attention.

If you're single, widowed, or divorced, you alone are responsible for the financial direction you pursue. If you marry, or remarry, your allocation of income, assets, and expenses may change. Assessing your current financial condition prepares you for possible changes, either personal or financial.

If you are planning with a partner, frequent discussion and negotiation of finances may become necessary. Joint financial planning is a prerequisite for a financial future that both partners enjoy. Although one partner may be more active in managing certain details, both partners should share in the decision making. The ability to give and take, indicative of a couple's ability to cooperate and compromise, improves the financial planning process.

Be wary of one partner determining financial direction or dominating the details of your joint financial decisions. Everyone knows someone who died or divorced, leaving a partner with little or no knowledge of their own assets or liabilities. Good planning can't be done in a vacuum. Share financial information with your partner.

If an active role doesn't come naturally, try to develop an interest and a more active role in understanding your financial situation. Become aware of the savings plans and pension plan options offered by not only your employer but also your partner's employer. Knowing the steps necessary to obtain your benefits means greater independence and self-confidence. Knowing what you have invested and what you can expect to receive in the future helps you to plan more accurately.

Answer the following questions. If you have a planning partner, answer the questions as individuals, and then compare your answers. If answers vary, joint planning is even more important.

Assessing Your Financial Condition	*Yes*	*No**
1. Are you comfortable with your savings and investment mix given the current economy?	☐	☐
2. Do you know your current financial condition, assets and liabilities?	☐	☐
3. Is this information in writing, and is it reviewed every six months?	☐	☐
4. Do you have an up-to-date will?	☐	☐
5. Do you annually review its provisions?	☐	☐
6. If you are remarried, have you considered the inheritance implications of your will on children of previous marriages?	☐	☐
7. Do you feel you have the financial planning knowledge to meet your future needs?	☐	☐
8. Could you cover an emergency expense of $4,000?	☐	☐
9. Does your budget cover expenses and contribute to savings?	☐	☐
10. Do you have an IRA account, annuity, 401k or other tax- deferred savings plan?	☐	☐
11. Do you understand what Social Security will provide?	☐	☐
12. Do you know whether your major assets are in joint or separate ownership?	☐	☐
13. Do you have property ownership as joint tenancy or tenancy in common, and are you aware of the differences?	☐	☐
14. Do you have enough current information on investment options to make wise decisions?	☐	☐
15. As a couple planning together, are your incomes from jobs, investments, and savings enough to make you feel financially comfortable?	☐	☐

* *If three or more questions have been answered no, additional personal planning is advised.*

Five Common Mistakes

1. **Failing to Establish Financial Goals.** Planning is the first investment you need to make in establishing your financial goals for the future. Planning leads to action that should lead to achieving your goals. You can't begin too early, but it's never too late to begin. The variety of investments and changes in the financial area make it important to update and, in some cases, revise your plans. Be sure to define both your short- and long-range goals.

2. **Losing Control of Financial Records.** Consistency is the key to maintaining control of financial records. Although it is sometimes tedious and repetitive, diligent and regular attention to detail pays over the long haul. Time and effort wasted in locating and reconstructing records can be more productively spent. Being aware of your assets and liabilities helps you to maintain control of your financial position.

3. **Reserving Insufficient Emergency Funds.** When everything is going well, it's hard to imagine a time of tight budgets and strained nerves. Things happen, however, and a reserve fund is absolutely the best insurance you can have. The distant future is today when unexpected events occur. Invest wisely, but remember to keep sufficient funds — three to six months of your gross income — available for an emergency. Such liquidity is essential when you need funds.

4. **Borrowing on Unfavorable Terms.** Some people get into debt trouble because of careless management or bad habits. Even if you have the skill to manage your income, compulsive spending and high-interest credit cards can get you into trouble. Borrowing can sometimes be the answer to college costs, mortgage investments, new cars, and appliances. However, educated consumers use caution when considering the terms of a loan or the rates on credit cards. Shop for low interest rates and reputable lenders.

5. **Investing without Investigating.** The old saying "If it sounds too good to be true, it probably is" still holds true. Use sound judgment and seek advice from experts with experience when considering an investment. Check references, make calls, and ask questions. It's your money; don't hesitate to find out the risks involved as well as the rewards expected. An investment that makes money for three years can just as easily suffer a reverse and lose everything in a year. It might take more than you

initially invested just to break even. If you invest for income, growth comes naturally.

Simply Do It . . . Save!

Andrew Tobias, one of the nation's foremost financial writers, said, "Becoming a nation of savers instead of a nation of spenders is one of the most important things we can do." He advises that we not get hung up on the fine points, agonizing over the absolute smartest place to invest your money or the precise right amount to save. The main thing, as with exercise, is simply to do it. Increase your rate of saving! Uncertain economic times and changing business policies make personal savings more important than ever. The 25 year consumption binge is ending, and in 2012, the US saving rate approached 5¼ percent. That is a dramatic shift brought about in large part by the "great recession". You can't invest your way to success…everything begins with savings.

Living Paycheck to Paycheck

Half of Americans have saved less than $2,500. How long do people say it would take for them to fall behind in bill payments?

26%	Immediately
28%	1 to 3 months
16%	4 to 6 months
6%	7 to 12 months
16%	Over 12 months
8%	Not sure

Source: Yankelovich Partners for Lutheran Brotherhood

Consumer Purchases	2004	2006	2012
Single-family Home	$182,500	$220,000	$161,000
Toyota Camry	$19,685	$21,200	$22,050
Unleaded Gasoline (gallon)	$2.27	$2.61	$3.35
A Year in College (private)	$16,638	$22,218	$27,143

Consider doing anything you can to lower your taxable income. Investigate tax-deferred investments to make the most of compounding. In addition to your 401k, thrift savings plan or IRA, consider tax-deferred municipal bonds and bond funds.

The simplest, least painful way to save is to have funds taken directly out of your paycheck. You don't take physical possession of the money, and without money in hand, you spend less on items you think you need but don't; or want but can't afford.

The Impact of Inflation

Inflation is a big factor in planning for your financial future. The cost of goods and services can vary widely from year to year. Even the moderate 3 percent inflation rate we've witnessed over the past few years has an impact on both your income and your investments. To combat inflation, consider a broad array of investment and savings options. Be sure that your savings plan earns more than the inflation rate.

As you do investment and financial planning, don't disregard the fact that a higher inflation rate may return. If it does, it will affect your investment choices. To understand how inflation erodes purchasing power, divide the projected annual inflation rate into 72. For instance, dividing a 4 percent inflation rate into 72 ($72 \div 4 = 18$) gives you 18. This means that in 18 years the purchasing power of your income is cut in half. A 6 percent inflation rate cuts your purchasing power in half in only 12 years.

Rule of 72 — Inflation

72	÷	the inflation %	=	years required to cut your $ in half
72	÷	4%	=	18 years
72	÷	6%	=	12 years

The President, Congress, the Federal Reserve Board and consumer spending all have an impact on inflation. What will the inflation rate be? At best, it's a guessing game. Inflation, however, will be with us in one form or another, and planning for it is one of the keys to your successful financial future.

Deflation

Deflation, in essence, is falling prices. The impact of falling prices ripples across the economy. It can mean lost jobs and certain investments may rapidly lose their luster. Computers, digital cameras, LCD and Plasma TVs are prime examples of deflation's effects. So is housing. Home prices in many U.S. markets dropped 25 to 35 percent between 2006 and 2012. If people feel prices will continue to drop (i.e., a deflating spiral) then they hold off on purchases, which ripples through all aspects of our economy.

The last time our country experienced severe deflation was during the Depression of the 1930s. The net impact of deflation on investments is that stocks, and often real estate, decline in price. Government paper, treasury bills, notes, bonds, and cash are the best places to be, in general, if we have a deflationary cycle. This would also be true of some high-grade municipal bonds. Most economists don't expect us to move into a deflationary spiral similar to the 1930s. Moderate deflation, however, has occurred in some areas of the economy. As you look at your asset allocation, keep the effects of deflation in mind.

The Power of Compounding

The earlier you begin a savings program, the more your savings accumulate. Most job-related benefit plans offer excellent opportunities for retirement savings with tax-deferred compounding. Since interest is compounded, investments made early in life may actually out-perform larger investments made later.

To understand how compounding works, we again take an interest rate and divide it into 72 (Rule of 72). In the inflation projection, you used the Rule of 72 to see when the purchasing power of your income is cut in half. In the power-of-compounding projection, you apply the Rule of 72 to see how long it will take for your money to double. For instance, dividing a 6 percent interest rate into 72 (72 ÷ 6) gives you 12. This means that in 12 years your money doubles; 8 percent interest means that in nine years your money doubles.

Rule of 72 — *Compound Interest*

72	÷	the interest rate	=	years required to double your money
72	÷	6%	=	12 years
72	÷	8%	=	9 years

The earlier you begin saving, the more powerful compounding becomes. Let's say at age 25 you begin saving $200 per month in an IRA, and that it earns 9%. Your boss Bob, who is 45, begins investing in the same IRA as you, but puts in $400 a month. Like you, he to earns 9% per year interest. At age 65, both will have invested $96,000. You will have $884,000, and Bob will have $616,000 that is $268,000 less. That's because you began 20 years earlier and took advantage of the miracle of compounding interest.

How much do you need to save to have a secure retirement? The answer is as much as you can and as early as you can! Most financial planners say 70% to 80% of your working income is a good target. Your Social Security and pension benefits combined may not be enough to meet your retirement living costs. You have more responsibility for financing your retirement than workers in earlier generations had. The reality of our changing workplace means that fewer people will retire after careers of 30 years with one organization. Planning now for the likelihood of funding your own retirement is very smart. It's possible to build wealth with dividend-paying stocks, bonds, and other income investments, thanks to the power of compounding.

The keys to this wealth-building strategy:

1. Don't consume the interest, and
2. Reinvest the interest automatically in an interest-earning account.

Strategies for Paying for College

An important part of your mid-career financial planning may involve saving for your child's education. Education can be a key to financial security, and it will continue to play an important role in our children's lives. Of course, learning in the 21st century costs more. The cost of higher education is rising yearly, with increases running well ahead of inflation. Advance planning is essential. To meet this challenge, you must invest early and regularly.

Experts suggest families begin planning as early as possible for these costs. The earlier you start building a college fund, the more affordable your monthly investments will be. Although you generally have only four years to pay for your child's college education, you do have up to 18 years to prepare. It's never too late, however, to begin a college investment program.

College Savings Plans

Methods of financing college have changed. Some colleges have pre-funding campaigns for future enrollees. The biggest change is the growth of 529 plans. These are investment plans operated by one of the states. The 529 plan has two general forms: **prepaid tuition plans** and **college savings plans**. Prepaid tuition plans allow you to pay in-state tuition or transfer the value to private/out-of-state schools. You may not, however, get full value if you choose to transfer. The full value of a college savings plan can be used at any accredited institution in the country. There are tax benefits with either option.

Gains accumulated in a 529 plan are exempt from federal taxes when withdrawn to pay for college. That one feature is enough to make them the best alternative for parents concerned about their children's higher education. If you select a 529 plan in your own state, it may also be exempt from state taxes. The popularity of 529 plans has exploded in the last few years. Most financial service firms now offer a 529 plan. Be careful! Each state has its own rules and benefits available to residents investing in their home state's plan. Therefore, it is probably wise to look at your own state's plan first, and then shop the market.

The attributes of a 529 plan extend beyond the potential of tax-free growth for college funds. There are no income limits or age limits for funding these plans; and more importantly, you stay in control of your account, not your beneficiary. That is critical. Before 529 plans were introduced, many people funded their children's college education through a Uniform Gift to Minors account, which technically became the child's when they reached the age of majority in their state (typically 18 or 21). How many 21-year-olds, receiving $20-, $40- or $50,000, are mature enough to use the money wisely?

Many plans allow you to contribute up to $200,000 per beneficiary. That's a lot of money. If you are wealthy and your child is considering a private school, those large contributions will come in handy. If, however, you are like the rest of us, and simply are looking for the best vehicle to save a couple of thousand or as much as you can a year, it would be wise to consider a 529 Plan.

Here are other ways to save for college:

1. Forming a trust is one way to transfer assets to your child. Although tax reform reduced some of the advantages, this strategy may enable your money to grow faster than if you held the assets in your name. College trust funds, however, are irrevocable and require you to give up control of the money. If you decide a trust may fit your needs, consult an attorney or the trust department of your bank.

2. Consider zero coupon investments that pay principal and all interest at maturity. Although a zero coupon bond pays no interest until its maturity date, the buyer knows exactly how much it will be worth at maturity. Buy bonds that mature during your child's college years so you'll know how much will be available.

3. Build assets for college with stocks and diversified stock mutual funds.

Strategic Borrowing

Get information; learn about financial aid. How do the college financial aid formulas calculate what you should be able to afford to pay, based on your family's income and assets? If you need to borrow money to cover college expenses, consider the special loans for education made through financial institutions. They are available to any creditworthy family facing college bills.

Consider these other options:

1. Many people borrow advantageously with home equity credit. Interest expense on your home equity loan up to $100,000 is generally fully tax deductible, and you can usually write checks as needed so that you avoid interest costs.

2. You may borrow from your employer-sponsored savings plan to pay college costs. This method of borrowing is tempting because most tax-deferred savings plans offer a more attractive interest rate than you can get from banks or credit unions. The interest rate may be lower than on a home equity loan, although interest payments are not tax deductible; and you must repay the loan within five years. In essence, you borrow from yourself and pay yourself back, but you are putting your retirement funds at risk of irrevocable depletion.

3. Certain newer types of life insurance combine life insurance protection with a tax-favored asset accumulation plan. You can borrow against the policy at a low net cost, and policy loans may even be tax-free in certain cases.

Strategic Investing

Financial planning experts suggest you begin planning as early as possible for rising college costs. Finding the right method for your family depends on your child's age, your family's resources and cash needs, and other considerations.

Sample College Investment Cycle

Birth to age 12	Buy shares in stock-owning mutual funds.
Age 12 to 14	Hold onto all past investments in mutual funds, but start putting new money into safer investments: Series EE Savings Bonds, Treasury securities, and certificates of deposit. Consider a balanced fund that divides your money between stocks and bonds.
Age 14	Move the freshman year money out of stocks and into a guaranteed four-year investment like a CD.
Age 15	Move out the sophomore-year money, and so on.

Before making a final decision, check with your legal or financial advisor to evaluate the long-term effect of various options on your financial planning.

Whom Do You Trust?

Trust is the single most important component in deciding where and with whom you place your investable income. If you wander into financial planning and the myriad investment options with inadequate preparation, trust becomes essential.

What can you do on your own?

A few years ago a national brokerage firm ran television advertisements with the theme of investing your time before you invest your money. Too often we don't want to learn ourselves; we simply want to delegate. Investing your time by first learning the financial planning ropes makes you a wiser investor. If you know what investments are being selected and why, you have more input in changing your strategy for better performance.

Non-credit investment classes for the general public are offered by local community colleges and universities. They are generic in nature and teach you the basic principles of cash planning and investment selection. Financial planning seminars are taught by brokers or planners in an attempt to develop a larger client base. Although they are sometimes forums for selling particular products, they can be helpful in giving you a broad overview of various investments. If you prefer learning on your own, go to the library and read current books and magazines on investing.

How do you find someone to advise you?

As mentioned earlier, invest your time before your money. Set your objectives before meeting with anyone. Decide your risk tolerance. Assess how much money you want to keep liquid and how much you can invest. Establish parameters for how much yield and return you want your investment to provide. Then you are ready to find someone to advise you. Seek people who have experience in the business and who have professional credentials. Does this mean you've got the best? No, not necessarily; but it does mean you'll be working with someone who has taken time to improve their knowledge and standing in their profession. Be prepared to review your total asset and liability picture. Don't be intimidated by the personal nature of the discussion. It is necessary that anyone helping you have knowledge of not only your objectives but also your investable amount of cash. The following designations represent different credentials in the investment community:

- A **Certified Financial Planner** (CFP) must have experience in the field, agree to a code of ethics, pass a comprehensive 10-hour exam, and have 30 hours of continuing education every two years. Some certified public accountants (CPAs) are also CFPs.
- **A Personal Financial Specialist** (PFS) must be a certified public accountant (CPA), pass an eight-hour exam given by the American Institute of CPAs, and have experience.
- A **Chartered Financial Consultant** (ChFC) must have a minimum of three years' experience in financial services (80 percent of the 25,000 ChFCs sell insurance) and pass 10 two-hour exams.

- A **Registered Investment Advisor** (RIA) must register with the Securities and Exchange Commission and is paid to give investment advice. This title involves no educational or experience requirements.

What kinds of questions do you need to ask?

Ask lots of questions. Here are seven to get you started.

- How many years of financial planning experience do you have?
- Given my age and assets, what would be your investment philosophy regarding risk and reward? i.e., how would you invest my money?
- Please provide me with three or four references of people with similar income who use your services.
- How are you compensated?
- What kinds of periodic feedback may I expect?
- What kind of advanced training have you had, and what type of financial designations do you hold?
- Most importantly — What do you need to know about me? (Make sure they ask you questions, lots of questions.)

It's your money! Finding an advisor you feel to be competent and trustworthy goes a long way to providing financial peace of mind.

How can you be sure your money is in good hands?

You can never be totally sure. You can, however, educate yourself so that you are an active, instead of a passive, partner in your own financial planning. If you know what's being done and why, and have developed an open, ongoing relationship with an investment advisor, you are more likely to monitor your funds. If you have good communication with those advising you, the odds of sounder investment strategies increase because you are both aware of the risk/reward relationships.

CHAPTER 3

Risk vs Reward

How can I take more risks without losing a bundle?
When do I sell versus waiting out a turnaround?
What do I need to understand about new investments?
How do no-load mutual funds charge for their services?
What does a well-balanced portfolio mean?
What is an appropriate retirement asset allocation mix?

I t is a difficult time to be an investor. What worked easily in the past isn't working as well today. Certificates of Deposit (CDs) and money market accounts now pay just a fraction of their former yields. High quality companies that a few years ago provided excellent growth potential now trade at new lows. Will markets continue to drop? Or is this the time to buy — when everything seems to be on sale? How can you gain an understanding of the basic principles of investing — principles that don't change — even though your investments may?

Different investments meet different objectives. Most people have five objectives when investing their money: safety, growth, yield, liquidity, and tax benefits. No one investment can meet all five objectives. Some safer investments provide a lower yield while high-growth investments may carry less safety. The key is to select a combination of investments that will give you the results you seek.

Your Investment Philosophy

Are you a risk taker? Or do you prefer safe investments backed by the federal government? Risk and reward are factors in all investment. The potential for greater return brings with it greater risk. Your investment philosophy reflects the level of risk with which you are comfortable.

All of your investments combined make up your portfolio. For example, your retirement savings portfolio may include a certificate of deposit in your IRA, equity investments in your 401k or thrift savings plan, and an annuity at an insurance company. Your investment philosophy influences the types of investments you choose.

Diversifying Investments

Diversification is distributing your funds among securities of different industries or classes. It is a method by which you, whether you have a small or large portfolio, can obtain your financial goals. Although there is no right way to invest, most investment professionals recommend diversification. It won't guarantee positive results, but it may help you achieve your goals, by spreading risk and lessening large-scale losses.

Allocating Assets

Asset allocation is distributing your investments among the three major asset classes — stocks, bonds, and cash equivalents. Choosing how your investments are split is a way of investing to fit your stage in life, your goals for the future, and your plans for retirement. Determining the allocation that works for you is critical to your investment success. Investment growth is primarily based on asset allocation and not on specific stock selection or market timing. For most investors, protecting your money while building assets means investing in vehicles such as stocks, bonds, and real estate or taking measured risks. Only you can decide how much of your investable cash to put into each type of investment; the decision is based on your goals and risk tolerance.

Stock Market

How long will a bull or bear market last? We can only guess. It's too risky to put money in or pull money out based on guesses. How long should you stay in the market? What about when the market is going down, or is flat for an extended period? One school of thought suggests buying quality investments with successful growth records and holding them for a long time. This buy and hold philosophy works better than the churn and burn, trading equities whenever the market is off or up by 10 percent.

Most people don't buy and hold forever. All investing requires careful monitoring, at least semiannually. If, however, you are saving for retirement, college funding, or a second home take a longer view to your investing.

To understand why buy and hold is recommended, look at time. The longer you hold equities, the less your risk of loss. If your time horizon is one year, your risk of loss is far greater than it is if you hold equities or mutual funds for five or 10 years. Business cycles usually occur in waves of four to seven years. The bull market of the 1990s was the longest on record. The market responds to a variety of factors, but normally, if you can stay in the market for five to 10 years, you minimize your losses because you ride out business cycles.

The Pyramid of Investment

The pyramid of investment offers a visual, structured approach to financial planning. A pyramid is built on a safe, solid foundation. Your financial future must also be built on a secure base provided by solid investments. After this base has been established more moderate risk investments can be considered. Investments in the base of the pyramid provide safety and liquidity. It is often suggested that between 45 and 60 percent of your investment dollars should be in conservative investments

HIGH RISK
Commodities
Options
Precious Metals
Investment
Real Estate
Global Funds

MODERATE RISK
Global Equity, Bond Fund
Mutual Funds
Small, Mid, Large Cap Equity Index Funds
Variable Annuities
Good Quality Corporate Bonds
Good Quality Stocks
Municipal Bonds

RISK

REWARD

CONSERVATIVE RISK
Fixed Income Tax Deferred Annuities
Certificates of Deposit
Series EE Bonds, I Bonds, Treasuries
Money Market Accounts & Funds
Cash-on-Hand
Insurance: Health, Life, etc.

as you approach retirement. The second section, the moderate risk investments, should contain between 35 and 45 percent of your investable income. As you move up the pyramid, investments involve increased risk; however, the potential for greater gains also increases. The high risk portion should generally contain no more than 5 percent of your money.

The closer you are to needing liquid assets, one to three years, the more conservative you want your investments to be. If you won't need the money for three to seven years, you can afford to take a more moderate approach. If you are more than eight years away from needing your money, consider more aggressive investments that produce higher returns.

Conservative Risk Investments

The lower section of the pyramid contains conservative risk investments. As you move up the pyramid, investments carry higher risk. Begin building your pyramid with a solid, well-thought-out foundation. The investments in this section are not slick and will not make money fast. Investments in the base section provide the structure you need before expanding your investment horizon. Most financial planners recommend gradually shifting some of your higher risk investments to more conservative areas as you approach retirement. By shifting away from higher risk investments, you reduce the potential for loss that could occur should you retire or need the money during a down market. One definition of loss is having to cash out of an investment at an inopportune time.

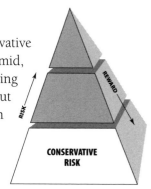

Insurance

Protecting your assets by insuring yourself and your family against catastrophe is fundamental to sound financial planning. Insurance on your life, health, home, and property is the cornerstone of most financial plans. Insurance takes many forms, from pure protection to serving as an investment vehicle. It is a contract between you and a company. You pay a relatively small cost, the premium, for sharing your risk with others facing similar risks. The cost of losses that occur is shared by all policyholders. Insurance products with investment options comprise 40 percent of all life insurance now sold.

Term Insurance. Term insurance provides simple death protection for a certain period and nothing more. There is no element of savings, and you cannot borrow against term insurance. Term insurance is usually calculated on a five- or 10-year renewable term with the option of renewing without an additional medical exam. Newer term policies often can provide a level term policy for up to 20 or 30 years. Policies may be convertible or non-convertible. A convertible policy may be exchanged for a higher premium whole life policy without a medical exam.

- Premiums for **level term** insurance increase at the end of every term, usually five, 10, 15, or 20 years, if the original face value of the policy remains the same.

- With a **decreasing term** policy, premium payments remain the same, but the face value of the policy decreases.
- Your employer most likely has **group term** coverage for you. Check to see if you can continue partial coverage in retirement. It could save you money.

A **Whole Life** policy agrees to pay a stated sum of money to your beneficiaries at your death. The premium usually remains level, building a cash value against which you can borrow.

Variable Universal Life policies buy death benefit protection; the remainder is invested and pays a periodically adjusted rate that reflects market rates. Earnings on the investment portion are tax-deferred. If you pay enough to cover the death benefit portion, usually you do not have to stick to a set monthly payment schedule.

A **Universal Life with Investment Choices** is a hybrid policy with a death benefit portion and an investment portion. Unlike Variable Universal Life, you choose where to invest the investment portion. You make scheduled premium payments, and the policy value may fluctuate, depending on the performance of your investment.

An **Umbrella Policy** is inexpensive and provides protection against high-dollar liability claims, adding at least one million dollars to your personal auto policy, homeowner's liability policy, and sometimes boat or recreational vehicle policy. The policy picks up liability claims not covered by your underlying policy.

Emergency Funds and Cash on Hand

Everyone should have three to six months of salary in safe, easily accessible (liquid) investments. The reasons are obvious. If you lose your job, a spouse needs surgery, or a child needs financial assistance — and they will — these funds will be available. Where should you keep these funds? In the past people kept their money in passbook savings accounts. Most passbook accounts now pay only ½ - 1½ percent interest. Credit unions will, in all probability pay ½ to 1 percent higher. Money market accounts will typically provide an even higher rate of return. All are safe and liquid sources for an emergency fund.

Banks, brokerage firms, and mutual funds all offer money market accounts with no interest rate ceiling. The interest rate floats, changing daily, driven by economic events and broad markets. You can write checks against your available funds, making them very liquid as long as a minimum balance is maintained. You should shop for the highest interest rates. Typically, banks will pay a lower interest rate than mutual funds or brokerage houses. Different institutions offer different rates; investigate your alternatives.

Series EE Bonds and Treasuries

Not too long ago if you were a small investor seeking safety with decent rates of return you bought U.S. Savings Bonds just as your parents and grandparents had. You only needed $50 to get started and with bank interest rates low savings bonds were a good alternative. Series EE savings bonds yield a fixed interest rate. That's a big change and not a positive one. Rates will no longer rise or fall as they have in the past when floating rates changed every six months.

I Bonds have also had interest rates revamped. The I bond's total rate is now based on a fixed rate combined with an inflation rate based on changes in the consumer price index. Most small investors would now be well advised to explore broker-held money markets, short term CDs, or online banks' savings vehicles, which may offer higher returns. We may be experiencing the end of the savings bond era.

Treasury Bills, also called T-bills, help finance government obligations. They are issued in maturities of 13, 26, and 52 weeks. A minimum of $100 is required to purchase T-bills. You buy them on a discount basis, receiving the face value at maturity. T-bills can be purchased from brokerage firms, banks, savings and loans, or directly from the government through the Federal Reserve banks. The Treasury auctions three- and six-month bills weekly; and one-year bills monthly. The interest is exempt from state and local taxation.

Treasury Notes are longer-term investments than T-bills with maturities of two to nine years, depending on your choice and minimum investments. Notes with maturities of less than five years require a $5,000 minimum investment. Notes with maturities of five years and above require a $1,000 minimum investment. The Treasury auctions two-year and five-year notes on the last business day each month; three-year and 10-year notes are auctioned quarterly. Interest is paid every six months. At maturity your Treasury note must be redeemed by mail.

Treasury Bonds have the longest maturity of all Treasury investments. The 10-year Treasury bond has become the benchmark most investors will consider when looking at longer-term government debt. A $1,000 minimum purchase is required. Interest is paid semiannually. You can buy Treasury bonds at auction (August and February) directly from the government or a broker. Your local Federal Reserve Bank can open a Treasury direct account. All Treasury securities are booked electronically; there are no longer printed certificates.

You can buy inflation-protection bonds (10-year notes) for $1,000 and up. The principal goes up or down with inflation according to the monthly consumer price index while the interest rate holds steady. Interest is paid twice yearly. You are taxed yearly on gains in the principal, so these notes are better for tax-deferred accounts.

How Bonds React to Events

Inflation rises	price falls, yield rises, duration falls
The bond ages	price moves toward par, yield moves toward shorter term rates, duration falls
Bond is downgraded	price usually falls, yield usually rises, duration usually falls
Call becomes likely	price usually moves toward the call price, yield moves toward shorter term rates, duration falls
Principal payment	price falls, yield rises, duration rises slightly
Coupon payment	price falls, yield rises, duration rises slightly
Prepayment rate rises	price moves toward par, yield moves toward shorter term rates, duration falls

Certificates of Deposit

The certificate of deposit (CD) was designed with safety of principal as its chief priority, and yield secondary. CDs can be purchased from banks and brokerage houses. Almost all CDs now have varying maturities and interest rates. Interest rates are determined by the bank or savings and loan.

Tax-Deferred Annuities

Deferred annuities are contracts, issued by insurance companies, that have nothing to do with insurance. The rates are guaranteed by law, and the funds are put into a legal trust fund. The timeframe for annuities vary. The shortest is for five years. Most have a penalty for early withdrawal. If interest rates fall, most annuities have a limit on how much they may drop in a year. Deferred annuities are not subject to contribution limitations.

When stocks "tank," interest rates are low, and financial planners are scrambling for business, annuities become more popular. With markets falling and few places to take shelter, annuities were sold as a relatively safe haven in stormy economic times. Besides that, annuities usually pay the seller a hefty commission.

Annuities may, however, fit into some portfolios. Most annuities are tax deferred and, generally, there is no limit on the amount you can contribute. That's good, but unlike an IRA, a 401k, or the Thrift Savings Plan for federal employees, you don't get any tax deduction for your contributions. That's bad. Thus, tax-deferred annuities present a good news/bad news story. They do grow tax deferred but there is no tax savings appearing annually on your W-2.

Annuity income is fully taxed when you begin making withdrawals. Typically, you select when you want payments to begin. Like an IRA, you can begin payments as early as 59½ or you may delay them until later. Your next decision is how you want your annuities dispersed. You can select a variety of options and survivorship rights. These are probably your most important considerations.

Index Annuity is a variation on the traditional deferred fixed annuity. It pays interest tied to the performance of at least one stock market index (like the S&P 500). A cap limits how much you can earn each year. When you cash out, the account value of your annuity is compared with the insurance companies guaranteed minimum. This minimum is usually 87.5% of your premiums plus interest of 1% to 3%. You receive whichever is greater.

Immediate annuities, as the name implies, is a fixed immediate annuity that is annuitized immediately…there is no deferral period. It starts paying guaranteed lifelong income as soon as it is purchased. As our lifespan increases, this alternative can help if you are concerned about outliving your savings, and want to avoid riskier investments.

Annuities are marketed in two broad categories — fixed and variable. A *fixed* annuity pays a fixed interest rate for a set period. Be careful. Some annuity vendors will offer "teaser rates" for a year or two. When CDs are paying 3½ percent, a teaser rate of 6 percent can look good, until you realize it is only for one year and you still have to factor in commissions and loads. After the teaser rate ends, many annuities will have an interest rate floor of 2 or 3 percent. Many insurance companies that underwrite and market annuities are removing the guaranteed minimum interest rate on new annuity business.

Variable annuities place more responsibility for the annuities' performance in your hands. You select the stock, bond, or money market funds you want. If they are poor performers, so is your annuity. If you get fed up and decide you want to cancel your annuity, there are often surrender charges.

The best part of an annuity may be the guarantee of payments to you at a designated time. They can be a riskier proposition when fees and commissions are high. Interest rates on fixed annuities are low, the performance of variable annuities may be poor. Give a lot of thought to why you are considering an annuity and then shop around for low-load or no-load annuity products.

Moderate Risk Investments

The mid-section of the pyramid holds the most appeal for the majority of investors. These are the investments that you hear about on the evening news. Here you will find the latest Internet funds, real estate investments and corporate bonds. There are no hard-and-fast rules about how much of your investment dollars should be in moderate risk investments. Normally, once you have a firm foundation of savings, insurance, and lower risk investments, you may place between 35 and 45 percent of your assets in the moderate risk area. How much you allocate is a mix of your risk tolerance, your investment time horizon, and the return you want over the long haul.

Tax-Deferred Savings Plans

Congress has liberalized IRA regulations, increasing the annual contribution rate limits and providing a catch-up provision for workers over 50 who haven't saved as much for retirement. These changes affect both regular and Roth IRAs.

Individual Retirement Accounts

IRAs are found in both the conservative- and moderate-risk sections of the pyramid. An IRA is a container that can hold a wide variety of investments such as CDs, individual stocks, or mutual funds. The container keeps the investments tax-deferred until you access them, as early as 59½ or as late as 70½.

Single/Head of Household		Joint Returns	
Tax Year	Phase-out Range	Tax Year	Phase-out Range
2012	$57,000-67,000	2012	$91,000-111,000

Maximum Annual Roth/Traditional IRA Contributions

Taxable Years	Maximum Contribution
2012 and thereafter	$5,000

The IRA limit is adjusted annually for inflation in $500 increments. The phase-out refers to the income ranges when you begin to lose your IRA tax deductibility and when it is completely gone.

The Age 50 Catch-Up Provision. Individuals who are at least 50 years old by the end of the tax year have a deduction/contribution limit $1,000 higher. Thus, a 50-year-old in 2012 could contribute $6,000.

A penalty of 10 percent, plus regular federal income tax, is assessed on funds withdrawn prior to age 59½. You cannot use your IRA for collateral since a loan is a premature distribution of IRA funds. If you become disabled and need your IRA funds, they may be withdrawn without penalty. Your beneficiary also has access to these funds, without penalty, upon your death. IRA contributions must be made by April 15 of each year, even if you get a tax-filing extension.

An IRA rollover means that if you receive a lump sum payment from a qualified, tax-deferred retirement savings plan when you terminate employment or before retirement, the funds can be put in your IRA. You can roll these funds into your IRA without tax liability if certain conditions are met. Remember, IRAs are portable. They can be moved from banks to S&Ls or brokerage firms. After a transfer, the funds may not be moved again for one year.

IRA Comparison

	Deductible	Non-deductible	Roth
2012 maximum contribution per individual under age 50			
	$5,000	$5,000	$5,000
2012 Catch up			
	$1,000	$1,000	$1,000
Contributions			
	deductible	non-deductible	non-deductible
Income tax treatment			
	100% taxable as withdrawn	Amount over basis taxable as withdrawn	No tax if held over 5 years & owner is 59½
Withdrawals			
	10% penalty pre 59½	10% penalty pre 59½	Contribution tax free at any time, 10% penalty on earnings pre 59½
10% penalty exceptions			
	Death, disability, medical expenses exceeding 7.5% of AGI, equal payments, first-time home ($10,000), college	Death, disability, medical expenses exceeding 7.5% of AGI, equal payments, first-time home ($10,000), college	Non-taxable after 5 years: Death, disability, first-time home ($10,000) Taxable: Medical expenses exceeding 7.5% of AGI, equal payments, college
Distribution requirements			
	Age 70½	Age 70½	None

Roth IRA. The Roth IRA is more flexible than the traditional IRA. Contributions are not tax deductible, but earnings and principal can be withdrawn tax-free at retirement. Under certain circumstances, investors can withdraw money (before age 59½) tax-free and penalty-free.

The tax-free nature of earnings from a Roth IRA means it seldom makes sense to make nondeductible contributions to a traditional IRA when that person qualifies to make a nondeductible Roth IRA contribution. Roth increases parallel those of traditional IRAs as do the catch-up provisions for those over 50 years old.

401k. A 401k plan combines the attributes of an IRA and a pension plan. You contribute pretax earnings to a retirement investment fund. Your salary is reduced for tax purposes by the amount of the contribution, and taxes are deferred on both the contribution and interest earned. The maximum contribution changes yearly, and withdrawal restrictions are similar to those for IRAs. Most 401k plans allow you to decide how much of your earnings, with certain maximum ceilings, you want to contribute and where the money is to be invested. A 403b or a 457 plan, like a 401k, is tax-deferred and reduces your taxable income.

In 2012, the limit is $17,000. The limit will be adjusted annually for inflation in $500 increments. The 401k plans, like IRAs, have catch-up provisions available for those over 50.

Keogh. Keogh plans are retirement savings programs for the self-employed. You can be employed full- or part-time. You can contribute $30,000, or 25 percent of earned income, whichever is less, to your Keogh plan. These plans are allowed to be set up by partnerships but not by corporations.

Bonds

A bond is a debt instrument or an IOU. You loan your money to the government, a company, or a municipality and, in exchange, they give you a bond on which they pay interest. The bond is their agreement with you. Some bonds, like U.S. savings bonds or Treasury bonds, are backed by the full faith and credit of the U.S. government. They are as safe as Uncle Sam's ability to pay. Some, like junk bonds sold by companies with poor or uneven credit histories, are a toss of the dice. Bonds, as an asset class, are usually not purchased for growth but for interest income. The interest rate should be substantial enough to attract you for a long-term investment.

You may purchase bonds in two different ways: as an individual bond or as shares in a bond mutual fund. There is an initial minimum investment required when purchasing an individual bond. If you are interested in purchasing a municipal bond, brokerage firms typically require a $5,000 initial purchase. Corporate bonds may require a smaller initial outlay, but these may still be prohibitive for the smaller investor.

Bond Mutual Funds. In a bond mutual fund, you and other investors hold shares in a large group of similar bonds. Investment in a bond mutual fund achieves limited diversification in one asset class, and your initial investment is usually lower than when purchasing a single bond. Shares in U.S. Treasury bonds are sold through Government Bond Funds.

Municipal Bonds. Legislation restricts what is and what is not a tax-exempt government bond by defining categories of facilities qualifying for tax-exempt financing. Municipal bonds are sold by municipalities attempting to raise money for local projects such as airports, waterworks, and schools. They are typically free of federal taxes and, if you purchase them in your state, they are also free of state taxes. This makes them especially attractive for investors in higher tax brackets. Municipal bonds, although now somewhat less attractive due to lower tax brackets, are still a good tax-planning investment. General Obligation Bonds, the largest category of municipal bonds, are backed by the taxing power of the municipality issuing them.

Corporate Bonds. These bonds are offered by corporations to raise the necessary money for a company's growth. Maturity ranges from five to 30 years. They carry varying degrees of risk and interest rates. Purchasing a corporate bond guarantees that on a specific date, usually twice a year, you will receive a fixed interest payment. The principal is due when the bond is retired. Bonds are usually sold in $1,000 units and purchased for income. Bonds may not always outrun inflation, but if you can lock in high interest rates, you will have a strong income source during economically unstable times.

Junk Bonds. These are non-investment-quality bonds. Companies with poor credit history, or high levels of debt, sell junk bonds. The credit rating of many well-known corporations has been downgraded in recent years, and the debt instruments they sell are rated as junk bonds. A junk bond pays higher interest and represents greater risk.

Rating Bonds. Bonds are rated alphabetically from the highest to the lowest. The rating is more important than the company issuing the bond. The greater the risk, the higher the interest paid on bonds. Banks and brokerage firms consider bonds rated BBB or better to be investment quality.

Bond Ratings	Moody's	Standard & Poors
Highest quality	Aaa	AAA
High quality	Aa	AA
Upper medium quality	A	A
Medium grade	Baa	BBB
Somewhat speculative	Ba	BB
Low grade, speculative	B	B
Low grade, default possible	Caa	CCC
Low grade, partial recovery possible	Ca	CC
Default, recovery unlikely	C	C

Stocks

If you own shares of stock in a company, you have an equity or ownership position in that company. Funds that buy stocks are often called equity funds. The company's individual performance, general economic conditions, and Wall Street sentiment all influence a stock's price movement. Buy stock for its price appreciation and/or dividends. Stocks require management, and most people owning stocks, especially large blocks, do not easily forget their up and down movements. If Wall Street's daily fluctuations make you nervous, look for a more stable, long-term investment that requires less watching and worrying. Purchasing stocks is a calculated gamble based on luck, the economy, your knowledge, and of course, the dependability of your broker.

Exchange-traded Funds

Between 2000 and 2012 money flowing into exchange-traded funds (ETFs) has grown dramatically. These funds trade like stocks but look like index-tracking mutual funds. In 2012, there were 1,400 different varieties of exchange-traded funds. They tracked everything from large benchmarks like the S&P 500 (SPDR) to different market sectors like pharmaceuticals (HOLDRS Pharmaceutical), energy (SPDR Energy), technology (SPDR Technology). Some ETFs track geographic regions, countries, and styles. Many ETFs are now tied to bonds. The emergence of ETFs tied to a diversified basket of various commodities or hard assets is also occurring. These could include precious metals, energy, and agriculture.

Index	*Tracks ...*	*Symbol*
S&P 500	Standard & Poor's 500	SPDRTrust
MSCI EAFE	markets in Europe, Australia, Far East	ishares MSCI EAFE
Russell 2000	smaller companies, small cap stocks	ishares Russell 2000
SPP Utilities	S&P 500 utilities	SPDR Utilities

Direct Stock Purchase Plans

A generation ago, investing in the stock market meant purchasing individual company stock. The problem was that high-quality stocks are often too expensive to purchase multiple shares. There is, however, an alternative for the small investor wanting to own stock in market-leading companies. Almost 800 U.S. companies offer Direct Stock Purchase Plans to shareholders. When you purchase stock directly from a company that offers a dividend reinvestment plan (DRIP), you can reinvest your dividends.

> *There are more things in life to worry about than just money*
> *— how to get hold of it, for example.*
>
> Anonymous

Most DRIPs allow you to make optional cash payments to purchase additional shares. Buy high-quality stock and continue to purchase additional shares monthly/quarterly. This allows you to use dollar cost averaging. You invest a set amount of money at regular intervals, buying fewer shares when prices are high and more when prices are low. Dollar cost averaging won't guarantee a profit, but a disciplined program increases the odds that your average cost will be below the average market price. This is an excellent strategy for long-term growth.

Mutual Funds

A mutual fund offers investors a diversified portfolio of professionally managed investments. Dollar cost averaging is also a good way to buy mutual funds. Mutual funds are sold in three ways:

Load Funds — a 4 to 6.5 percent commission is charged to purchase load funds, plus an administrative fee of typically 1 to 2 percent.

Low-load Funds — a 2 to 4 percent commission is charged to purchase low-load funds, plus an administrative fee of .75 to 2 percent.

No-load Funds — no commission is charged to purchase no-load funds, but an annual administrative fee of 0.15 to 1.5 percent is charged.

After purchasing shares in a mutual fund, you can redeem them any time for their net asset value per share (the value of the fund's assets, divided by the number of outstanding shares). One of the most successful types of mutual funds has been a balanced fund. Balanced funds are a good way to diversify, and typically include stocks, fixed-income investments, and money market instruments.

Most investors considering mutual funds can use help in sorting through the numerous funds available and in understanding how funds are ranked. Mutual funds are ranked using basic variables, such as price change over a specified period; but the combination of variables used differs widely. When looking at mutual fund rankings, experts advise that you consider the following guidelines:

- Risk should be an explicit and important element in any ranking.
- Ranking should emphasize 5- to 10-year performance data. Shorter periods are less meaningful and longer periods may reflect changes in management and/or philosophy.
- Rank funds against other funds with very similar investment objectives.
- Don't rely too much on rankings in your analysis. Get a prospectus and annual report from top-ranked funds in the same category.

Fund Types

Balanced:	Invest in a mix of stocks and bonds
Emerging markets:	Invest in stocks in countries with small but growing economies
European region:	Invest in companies in Europe
Global:	Stocks around the globe — foreign and U.S., risk of currency fluctuation
Growth:	Stocks that should increase in price, focus is on future earnings potential
Health/biotechnology:	Invest at least 65% in health care, medicine, and biotech
Income:	Stocks/bonds paying dividends/interest; avoids risk by providing stable income
Index:	Attempts to duplicate stock and bond market indexes; strategy is buying the market
International:	Foreign stocks, risk of political instability and currency fluctuation
Large-cap:	Stocks of companies valued at $1 billion plus
Mid-cap:	Midsize companies with market value less than $5 billion
Natural resources:	Invest in stocks of natural-resources companies
Pacific region:	Concentrates on western Pacific basin companies
Science/technology:	Focus on stocks of science and technology companies
Sector:	Invest in a particular sector/industry, does not offer typical diversification
Small-cap:	Stocks of companies valued under $1 billion
Value:	Stocks with low PE ratios, more conservative than a growth fund approach

The summary-of-expenses table in every fund prospectus reveals the true cost of investing. All fee tables follow the basic format shown in the following table.

Transaction Expenses: *Fees you must pay when buying or selling shares*

Maximum charge	0 to 6.5%	The commission (load) usually imposed on broker-sold funds
Maximum charge	0 to 7.25%	Fee levied by a few broker-sold funds on automatically reinvested dividends
Deferred sales charge	0 to 6%	Charge imposed if you redeem your shares within 5 or 6 years; typically, the fee declines 1 percentage point for each year you own the fund
Redemption fee	0 to 2%	Charge paid on any withdrawals; usually expires within 6 months to a year
Exchange fee	0 to $10	Charge for switching from one fund to another transaction in the same family

Annual Fund Operating Expenses:
Fees deducted annually from the fund's holdings, expressed as a percentage of average net assets

Management fees	0.2% to 1.6%	Money paid to the investment advisor for managing the fund's portfolio
12b-1 fees	0 to 1.25%	Money used to pay a fund's distribution costs, including ongoing commissions
Other expenses	0.2% to 1%	Ordinary business expenses such as legal, printing, and accounting
Total operating	0.35% to 2.5%	Total of all the fund's annual cost expense

Index Funds . . . A Simple Way to Track the Market

Index funds are a simple way to ride the stock market. Whatever the market delivers in performance, both good and bad, index funds can provide. Buying index mutual funds is an inexpensive, tax-efficient way of buying broad exposure to the entire market or a particular market segment. Index funds have no active management, and that makes them cheap. These funds have become extremely popular because of their simplicity. You can purchase a variety of different indices that parallel various market segments and diversify investments.

The Background. Index funds have been in existence since the 1970s, but their phenomenal growth occurred in the 1990s due, in part, to the 1990 Nobel Prize. In 1990 the Nobel Prize in economics was awarded to Harry Markowitz, Merton Miller, and William Sharpe for their research into Modern Portfolio Theory, the philosophical basis for index funds. The theory suggests that investors will be more successful over time if they take a passive approach instead of an active, managed approach to their investing. Modern Portfolio Theory contends that trying consistently to beat the stock market is a losing game because of the expenses, fees, and taxes that are by-products of active, managed investing.

When most people think of index funds, they immediately think of the S&P 500; however, you can buy index funds that track almost 30 different equity and bond markets. There are more than 250 index funds. If you're interested in the non-U.S. stock market, seek funds that track the Morgan Stanley EAFE. If you're interested in small capitalization stocks, purchase an index fund that parallels the Russell 2000 index. Real estate stock investors who wish to own an index that broadly tracks a composite of real estate investment trusts would seek an index fund that tracks the Morgan Stanley REIT.

Taking Action. Keep it simple. The simplest action to take, with the best chance of long-run success, is investing in index funds. What type of index do you wish to benchmark? Are you interested in stocks, bonds, or real estate investment trusts? Do you wish to mimic the performance of all U.S. stocks or only the S&P 500? The Wilshire 5000 offers greater exposure to small, medium, and large companies than does the S&P 500. Begin by deciding what market, or market sector, you want to track. One index fund may not meet all of your long-range needs. Consider mixing and matching two or three different types to achieve a balanced portfolio.

Building a Foundation. After deciding your investment goals, time frames, and your risk tolerance, it's time to look at an investment strategy. Look at the pyramid of investment as a pyramid of index funds. Those in the base provide a foundation. Experts suggest building your foundation on stock market index funds. Those that mimic the Wilshire 5000 index provide exposure to large, midsize, and small company stock. It is broad-based and inclusive. This base is the foundation for investing in other types of index funds.

The upper layers of your pyramid provide opportunities to branch out into small capitalization stocks, foreign funds, and bonds. A beginning investor might build the foundation with 60 percent in a fund tracking the Wilshire 5000, 25 percent in a broad-based global stock index, and 10 percent in a bond index. Monitor it occasionally, and let it ride.

The key to success is keeping your eye
on those things you cannot see.
— *Japanese Proverb*

It's Not What You Make It's What You Keep. Keep in mind that all index funds are not created equal. As their popularity has grown, brokerage firms or commissioned mutual fund vendors have hopped on the bandwagon. Keep fees and commissions on index funds to a minimum, and keep a careful watch on the fees you are charged. The average index fund has an expense fee of .5 percent compared to almost 1.5 percent for a managed fund.

But shop around so your investment savvy isn't limited to index funds. Investing in index funds is not a 50-yard dash; it's a long-distance run. It can, and will, provide winning results if you stay in the race and keep your eye on the finish line. No other strategy offers the same benefits, simplicity, low cost, tax-savings, and performance.

International Investing

The international stock and bond market permits you to further diversify. Anyone looking at stocks or mutual funds should also consider global investments. Many investment alternatives access worldwide markets, and a global strategy may enhance your overall investment plan. Going global can be done conservatively, or it can increase your risk. Like the U.S. market, international stock and bond investments carry different levels of risk and reward. Look at how the investment has performed over the past five or 10 years before making a decision. A consistently strong performance usually indicates less volatility.

There are special considerations associated with international investing, including the risk of currency fluctuation, but it should play an important role in most investors' long-term financial plans. The Morgan Stanley Capital International-Europe, Asia and Far East Index (MCI-EAFE) shows the performance of world markets and the relative strength of most foreign currencies.

	S&P500	**MSCI-EAFE**
2006	15.79%	26.88%
2007	5.49%	24.6%
2008	-38 .50%	-42.8%
2009	26.68%	68.82%
2010	15.1%	4.9%
2011	-.003%	-10.26%

Source: MCI, Standard & Poor's and Bernstein

Higher Risk Investments

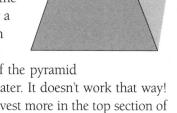

The top section of the pyramid contains investments that carry the highest risk. You can design a well-diversified portfolio without ever entering the top portion of the pyramid. In this area, the potential for loss is usually greater than the potential for gain. It is human nature to hear a tip on a hot stock and dump money into an investment hoping it will bring spectacular gains. Many of us want to start at the top of the pyramid looking for quick profits and fill in the rest later. It doesn't work that way! Use caution and common sense and never invest more in the top section of the pyramid than you are willing to lose.

Real Estate

Investment real estate is in the top section of the pyramid because of risk and the amounts of capital involved. This investment takes many forms: undeveloped land, vacation property, second homes, apartments, or office buildings. You can invest on your own or with others. There will always be demand for the right type of real estate. Will Rogers perhaps stated it best: "Invest in real estate because they ain't making it anymore."

Do you want to eat better or sleep better?

—J. P. Morgan

In any investment, always look at tax liability implications. This is especially true of real estate. Tax law changes have curtailed many advantages that real estate investments once had. Rental property is now depreciated straight-line over 27.5 years. Mortgage interest may or may not be deductible. Check with your accountant before investing in real estate.

A real estate investment trust (REIT), most often sold through brokerage firms, provides management advantages, eliminating headaches associated with managing your own rental property. Most REITs seek income instead of tax advantages.

Precious Metals

Gold, silver, and other precious metals are in the top section of the pyramid. Price fluctuations can be extreme with these investments. Although gold and silver produce no income until they are sold, many people hold precious metals for the feeling of security they provide in unstable times. Prices for precious metals are up as economic uncertainty in the U.S. continues.

Stock Options and Commodities

Stock options are contracts to buy or sell shares of stock. The price of the option increases or decreases as the price of the stock increases or decreases. There are two types of options, calls and puts. If you think a stock will rise in value over a specific period, you purchase a call, the right to buy at a given price. If you think the stock will drop in price over a specific period, you purchase a put, the right to sell at a given price. All options have specific maturities from one day to nine months. If you limit your option trading to buying options, your maximum risk is your investment in the options.

Commodity futures are contracts to buy or sell commodities — corn, wheat, or soybeans, etc. — at a future date. Extreme price fluctuations determine winning or losing. Use caution. Stock options and commodities are at the speculative peak of the investment pyramid of investment. *The New York Times* reports that as many as 85 percent of those investing in commodities lose money on their buy and sell decisions.

Staying the Course vs. Bailing Out

Over time stocks outperform all other asset classes. From the stock market crash of 1929 through 2011, stocks returned an average of 9 percent. It's how long is meant by *over time*, that causes some people concern. When the market crashed in October 1929, ushering in the Great Depression, you would have had to wait 24 years for the market to return to its 1929 peak. In the recession of 1973-1974, it took seven years and seven months for the stock market to return to its 1973 high point. So everything is contingent upon your time horizon — how long can you wait?

The chance of loss decreases the longer you are in the market. For instance, over the past 20 years the market declined in 36 percent of the months, 25 percent of the years, and 6 percent of the rolling 10 year periods. Put another way, the longer you are investing, the smaller the chances are that the market declines.

Deciding if and when to sell a stock or mutual fund as it falls in value is very difficult. There's an old financial planning saying that if you find a stock interesting at $50, you're in love at $30 and married to the bitter end at $10. Selling is always harder than buying because we're loss averse. We want to recoup our losses . . . often you simply can't.

There are no easy answers as far as when to dump the dogs. There are, however, common sense guidelines. Are the reasons you own a particular stock or fund still as valid today as the day you purchased it? Are the fundamentals still sound? Has the company or fund undergone management change, change in business strategy, increased competition, or a shift in market conditions? How have they responded? If the company fundamentals remain strong, and you are as comfortable owning the stock in difficult times as you were buying it, then trust your gut and hang in for the long run.

How long does a typical recession last? The general definition of a recession is two consecutive quarters of negative growth. The average recession lasts approximately 18 months. Over the last 30 years, the depth and length of recessions varied greatly. The reasons lie at the heart of what caused the recession and kept us in a recessionary economy.

Public psychology has a great deal to do with the length of a recession.

Almost 80 years ago, Franklin D. Roosevelt rallied the country with "The only thing we have to fear is fear itself." Indeed, public fear and the economic paralysis it causes is sometimes the biggest obstacle to overcoming a recession.

Date	Event	Time to...	Maximum decline	Time to recover
10/24/29	Depression	1,000 days	-86.5%	8,910 days
12/07/41	Pearl Harbor	142 days	-20.3%	341 days
10/22/62	Cuban Missile Crisis	1 day	-1.85%	2 days
10/17/73	Oil Embargo	425 days	-40.29%	820 days
11/04/79	Iran Hostage Crisis	3 days	-2.71%	6 days
10/19/87	Stock Market Crash	1 day	-22.61%	455 days
08/05/90	Gulf War	67 days	-15.82%	185 days
04/19/95	OK City Bombing	unknown	unknown	unknown
09/11/01	9/11 Terrorist Attack	9 days	-5.7%	85 days
12/07	Sub Prime Lending Crisis	1 yr. 4 mos.	-53.4%	Unknown

What can I do to protect my retirement income? Diversify, diversify, diversify. Don't put all your eggs in one basket. The importance of diversification was driven home by investors who had the majority of their investments in the tech-heavy growth era of the late 1990s, or the amazingly strong financial sectors in 2006-2007. Both of those sectors tumbled badly. Spread your risks among cash and cash equivalence, bonds and stocks. Another tool often used is to shift some of your equity investment to fixed income or cash equivalents as you approach retirement. Begin this process five to 10 years prior to retiring. If loss can be defined as having to cash out at an inopportune time, then shifting funds toward more conservative areas before retirement is prudent. That way you're protecting your future by reducing risk. Do this gradually, it works better that way.

Keep in mind that most people will always want some money in equities. A guideline: subtract your age from 110. Thus, a 48-year-old (110 – 48 = 62) should theoretically have 62 percent of his or her investable income in equities. At 68 that percentage would drop to 42 percent. Most of us don't plan on living as long as we will. For that reason, equities in whatever percentage you feel is appropriate should be a part of your retirement portfolio.

CHAPTER 4

Documents and Decisions

Should I set up a trust for my beneficiaries?
What is a living will, and will it be honored?
Is just having a will enough?
Which types of property ownership have survivorship rights?
Is probate a problem?

You've spent a good part of your life saving for the future and providing for your family's well-being. Protecting your family and distributing your financial assets and property, according to your wishes, are the most important reasons for preparing legal documents. This chapter addresses some of these often neglected legal issues.

Why Estate Planning?

Your estate includes everything you own less everything you owe. Few people plan adequately for what happens to their estates at death. Lack of planning can result in higher taxes, higher probate costs. You think that your estate is too small to require planning? You would be surprised at how large an estate you actually have once you begin totaling assets: your home, insurance policies, cars, stocks, bonds, real estate, retirement benefits, profit-sharing, and stock-purchase plans. Everyone with income or property should be concerned with estate planning. It can save thousands of dollars in unnecessary costs.

Estate planning includes:
- Accumulating assets
- Preserving assets
- Disposing of assets

An estate planning team often consists of an attorney, a life insurance agent, an accountant, and an investment advisor or bank trust officer. Using this team allows you, or your attorney, to develop an estate plan that covers not only drafting a will but also tax issues, insurance, and investments. Estate planning objectives should include provisions for your spouse and children at your death. A gift program can be established regarding personal property, residences, and specific bequests. Gifts to your favorite charities and any special considerations or instructions can be covered in your estate plan. Consider your retirement objectives, and make these goals a part of your estate planning.

A Legal Planning Checklist	*Yes*	*No*
1. Do you have a will?	☐	☐
2. Do you review it every two years?	☐	☐
3. Does your spouse have a will?		
4. If you own a life insurance policy, do you understand its provisions?	☐	☐
5. Do you understand the benefit provisions of your pension plan?	☐	☐
6. Are your assets owned jointly?	☐	☐
7. Do you currently have an attorney?	☐	☐
8. Have you considered establishing a power of attorney should you be temporarily incapacitated?	☐	☐
9. Have you considered setting up a trust for beneficiaries of your estate?	☐	☐
10. Do you have a general understanding of how your estate may be taxed at your death?	☐	☐
11. If you have remarried, have you made a new will?	☐	☐
12. If you're contemplating marriage, have you considered a prenuptial agreement?	☐	☐

Put documents in place now, designating your wishes. You may want to include telephone numbers — your pension and health plan administrators, the Social Security Administration, the IRS and your accountant — so your survivors can get information quickly on taxes, required reports, etc. If you are a veteran, include the Veteran's Administration for questions about benefits.

Wills and Power of Attorney

A will is the cornerstone of estate planning, yet more than two-thirds of Americans are without a will. Every man or woman, married or single, should have an estate plan, including a properly drafted will. Even if you and your spouse are joint property owners, each should have a will. It is planning for your peace of mind and that of your heirs.

Some people believe that, will or no will, your surviving spouse gets the estate at your death. This isn't always the case. Laws vary from state to state.

Emergencies don't wait for you to get your legal house in order!

In many states a surviving spouse with two children and no will receives one-third of the estate and each child gets one-third. If there are no children, the spouse, in some instances, shares the estate with parents and siblings of the deceased. If you die intestate (without a will), your property will be distributed according to state law. Your wishes and the needs of your heirs may not be considered. Drafting a will most often includes the following steps:

- Naming an executor and alternate executor to handle property distribution
- Choosing a guardian for children if you and your spouse should die
- Setting up a trust fund for your wife/husband and/or children
- Naming recipients of valuable (or valued) possessions
- Designating charitable contributions
- Considering estate tax reduction strategies

Some attorneys will draft a simple will for under $400. This type of will usually leaves the entire estate to the surviving spouse. It is straightforward, uncomplicated. Today consumers are also turning to the web for legal advice. You can download a will kit from at least a dozen different web sites promoting inexpensive wills designed with your state's laws in mind.

These are just simple wills. Anything more detailed requires a visit with an attorney.

A more complicated will leaves your estate to your spouse with a contingent trust set up for minor children, if your spouse does not survive. If your estate is large, and taxes are a problem, a marital deduction will might be a wise consideration. This will is written with a residual trust so some benefits flow to the surviving spouse. Assets are placed in a trust that should escape taxation when your spouse dies. The assets in the trust then go to your children or whomever you designate.

Health Care Directives

A health care directive is a written declaration, directing a doctor or health care provider not to apply heroic or extraordinary means of treatment for a terminal illness, thereby permitting natural death. The information must be precise, state clearly what you want, as well as what you don't want, thereby maintaining control of your own destiny. About 90 percent of state legislatures have approved health care directives, and many local medical societies will send you a living will form free of charge. Think of health care directives as an upgraded living will. It takes the decision to continue/discontinue extraordinary treatment, like life support, and puts it in the hands of someone you designate, a spouse or family member. It's often better than a living will. Your loved one knows your wishes at a time when you may not be able to communicate them.

Tasks of an Executor

The tasks that an executor of an estate must perform may vary somewhat from state to state, but they will also have much in common. Many of the tasks will depend on what the will provides, as well as on the type of assets in the estate.

- **Preliminary Steps.** Locate and study the will. Confer with an attorney.
- **Assemble, Inventory, and Protect Assets.** List the contents of all safe deposit boxes; locate all property, real and personal; analyze business interests (whether to continue, liquidate, or sell), and arrange for interim management.
- **Study Financial Records.** Send death notification to all insurance companies; make a comprehensive study of the financial and business interests of the deceased in the years immediately prior to death; study

employment contracts or any deferred compensation plans to determine whether or not payments are due to the estate.

- **Administer the Estate.** File federal preliminary estate tax notice; notify banks, investment brokers, and others of appointment as executor; close bank accounts and transfer cash to estate; inspect real estate, leases, and mortgages; have assets appraised; transfer assets to estate; file claim for Social Security or veteran's benefits; collect income, accounts receivable, and other funds owed the deceased or estate; keep beneficiaries informed of the progress of the estate settlement.

- **Determine Personal and Estate Tax Liability.** Estimate cash needed for estate settlement; select assets for sale to provide needed cash; file income tax return for the deceased; prepare for audit of income tax returns previously filed by the deceased; determine whether beneficiaries who receive property outside the will shall be required to pay their share of the death taxes; secure federal estate tax release so that distributions may be made as promptly as possible.

- **Distribute the Estate and Make Final Settlement.** In distributing assets from a residuary estate, choose a date that results in the best tax treatment for the beneficiaries as well as the estate; prepare information for the final accounting, including all assets, income, and disbursements; secure releases from beneficiaries and, in some states, discharge from the court.

Powers of Attorney

A **power of attorney** is a document authorizing another individual to act on your behalf. This includes taking action on any personal business that requires your signature or presence. The authority can be limited to certain areas or grant complete authority. That decision is yours. All states now provide that a properly drafted power of attorney will be effective even in cases of the disability or incapacity of the person who gave the power of attorney.

Trusts

A trust is a way to turn over assets to someone else. The trustee (holder of the property) holds legal title and accepts all management responsibility of the trust for the beneficiary. Trusts can be revocable or irrevocable. They can be established and effective during your life (*inter vivos trusts*) or at your death (*testamentary trusts*). Revocable trusts become irrevocable if trustees die or become mentally incapacitated. Wealthy people have used the tax advantages of trusts for years, but trusts are also for average income people who want the advantages a trust provides. Parents often use trusts to prevent immature young adults from rapidly depleting their inheritance. A trust may specify, for instance, that the inheritance be distributed in thirds at specified ages. Trusts can provide an income stream for aged parents or charities. If you decide a trust may fit your needs, consult an attorney or the trust department of your bank.

Living Trusts

A living trust protects your estate while you're alive and also can continue after your death. This is a legal arrangement that requires an agreement between you, the owner, and the trustee. The trustee can be a relative, a trusted friend, or bank trust department; it can also be you, as initial trustee. The beneficiary of the trust can be anyone you designate. A living trust is activated while the owner is alive.

Under a will, an estate is settled in probate court. There are lawyers' fees and court costs. The proceedings are a matter of public record, and substantial time can elapse before the estate is fully settled. A living trust, however, is settled without the cost and public nature of a court proceeding. A successor trustee distributes assets according to the instructions of the trust, with an accountant, notary public, or lawyer certifying any transfer of titles. The process is faster, less expensive, and more private. Trusts, like wills, can be contested; but a will is generally more easily contested by an unhappy heir than a trust. If you think the living trust might meet your specific estate planning needs, consult an estate planning attorney. There are two types of living trusts: revocable and irrevocable.

You cannot change an *irrevocable living trust* after it is established. The benefit is that it continues to be managed as you intended if you become unable to handle your finances.

A *revocable living trust* allows you to revise the terms of the trust as your financial situation or family needs change. The benefit of this type of trust is that you avoid probate, may possibly save on estate taxes, and you maintain access and control of the assets held in trust. Naming yourself as trustee allows you to continue to control your assets. The major disadvantages to a revocable living trust involve the time and effort required to transfer the titles to homes, bank accounts, securities, businesses, and other assets into the trust. Refinancing a home that is part of a trust may require removing the home from the trust and, after refinancing has been accomplished, transferring it back into the trust.

Other Legal Issues

Your future is not predictable. Many events that will happen to you and your family will be totally unexpected. Others, however, have a higher probability and an ounce of planning is always worth a pound of regret.

Planning with Aging Parents

Like many people you may find it hard to think beyond the lifetime of your parents and harder still to discuss estate planning issues with them. Make things easier for yourself and for your parents by ensuring that they have the necessary documents prepared. If you have brothers or sisters, encourage them to be involved in these discussions from the beginning. Help your parents prepare six basic documents:

1. A will that names a trustee or executor
2. Power of attorney
3. Durable power of attorney for health care
4. A living will
5. A letter of instruction to heirs
6. An inventory of finances

Organize financial records and information that you'll need when your parents can no longer make decisions for themselves. These are important issues for you to consider in possibly caring for an aging parent sometime in the future.

Property Ownership

Joint tenancy is ownership of property by two or more people; the major advantage is survivorship. It is a way in which two or more persons may hold title to property in equal, undivided shares. When one owner dies, his or her share of the property is not passed on according to a will, but automatically becomes the property of the surviving joint tenant(s). If you and I own property as joint tenants, and I die, my interest automatically goes to you, my survivor. When husband and wife jointly own property, it is called tenants by the entireties. This form of ownership exists only between husband and wife. Upon the death of either joint owner, the survivor automatically becomes the owner.

When property is owned by two or more people without the right of survivorship, it is called tenancy-in-common. When two or more people own property, each is the sole owner of his or her share. Upon one owner's death, the property is a part of his or her estate and can be passed on by will, or under state law if there is no will. Tenancy-in-common, however, does not establish a survivorship interest as joint tenancy does. If you and I own property as tenants-in-common, and I die, my interest in the property goes to my estate, not to you.

Joint ownership is an unwise substitute for a will. When husband and wife place substantial sums in joint ownership, estate taxes may be needlessly expensive, and property can possibly go to unintended heirs. Without a valid will, an estate must be distributed according to state laws. Therefore, check with your attorney about the laws in your state.

Estate Taxes

Federal estate tax is the tax that beneficiaries pay on inherited assets. The tax is applied to all property owned at a person's death and even certain property transferred during one's lifetime. The top tax rate is 35 percent, with an exemption of five million per individual for 2012. Congress deferred a tough decision until 2013, when they will again have to address this.

Taxable estates can be reduced by the marital deduction, which lets an individual leave any amount of property to a spouse, tax free, avoiding the estate tax until the death of the surviving spouse. This may, however, increase the tax paid on the second estate.

An estate's assets can be reduced with a lifetime gift program. By law, you can give each heir up to $13,000 tax free, each year. Your spouse also can give up to $13,000, for a total of $26,000 to be given to any one heir per year with no gift tax ramifications. In addition to this annual exclusion, you may also exclude sums paid directly to educational institutions for tuition or to a medical facility for health care.

Year	Estate Tax Limit	Tax Rate	Gift Tax Limit	Tax Rate*
2012	$5 million	35%	$1 million	35%

* The gift tax rate is equal to the highest income tax rate in effect for the year in which the gift is made. Currently that is 35 percent.

Many states impose a "sponge" estate tax to take advantage of the maximum amount that otherwise would be paid in federal estate taxes, instead of having their own estate tax. The act repeals the state death tax credit, depriving states of that tax revenue. This will add to the revenue problems already facing most states due to the economic slowdown, and could result in states enacting their own inheritance taxes.

Currently, the strategies being most widely applied focus on flexibility and the willingness to consider disclaimers and other postmortem techniques. Except for the rare instances when a taxpayer is able to predict his or her own death, it is no longer possible for tax advisors to provide clear estimates of the taxes that will be due — on even modest wealth.

If you expect to pass on a larger estate, consult an attorney specializing in tax and estate planning. It makes sense to spend a little money on advice now to avoid a potentially large tax burden for your heirs.

Learning More

To find out more about the laws in your state, there's plenty of information on the web. Before you begin your search, you need to be aware that laws are different in each state, particularly real estate laws.

Doing legal research on the Internet is fine. Many sites provide legal information. If you are looking for free legal advice, however, beware. Even when you find an answer to your question, it's a good idea to look at more than one site to be sure the answers are consistent. Look for a name behind the web address and information on who is writing the articles or running the site. Look for the last date that the information was updated to be sure the information is current. Laws change, and what is correct today may not be valid tomorrow.

One of the largest Internet legal sites, **findlaw.com**, has links to commercial and institutional sites, including bar associations for every state. The American Bar Association's site, **abanet.org**, has links to local bar associations and a directory of lawyers. The site **lawguru.com** has links to statutes, the Constitution, and other legal sites for every state and territory, along with a password-protected search engine. Find user-friendly explanations of basic legal issues on **freeadvice.com**, which also has "I want a lawyer" links under every heading. The Internet is a great place to begin learning and to collect preliminary advice. Just as with obtaining financial advice you should invest your time before you invest your money. It is one thing to buy the latest toy for your child online, and quite another to prepare your legal documents that way.

You need to understand that there is wide variation in the quality of web sites, legal and otherwise. The Internet gives equal billing to law libraries and ambulance chasers. Choose carefully; and remember, your Internet advisor probably won't be able to argue for you in court if it becomes necessary.

Common Legal Terms

Administrator: An individual or trust institution appointed by a court to settle the estate of a person who has died without leaving a valid will.

Amortization: A loan payment consists of two portions: one applied to the principal and the other applied to the interest. As the loan balance decreases, the amount applied to interest decreases and the amount applied to principal increases so the loan is paid off, or amortized, in the specified time.

Codicil: An amendment/supplement to a will, requiring execution with the same formality.

Common Trust Fund: A fund maintained by a bank exclusively for the collective investment and reinvestment of the assets of numerous small trusts.

Contingency: A condition that must be met before a contract is legally binding.

Corpus: The principal body (capital) of an estate, as distinguished from the income.

Custodian: Person who controls an asset gifted to a minor under the Uniform Transfers to Minors Act. The custodian may only use the asset for the benefit of the minor, and the minor is entitled to take over control at age 21.

Deed of trust: Some states do not record mortgages. Instead, they record a deed of trust, which is essentially the same thing.

Executor: A person or trust institution named in a will and/or appointed by a court to handle the settling of an estate.

Guardian: An individual or trust institution appointed by a court to handle the affairs of a person who is physically or mentally incapable of taking care of his/her own affairs.

Health Care Representative: Your agent, usually a spouse, child, or other close relative familiar with your health care wishes, who can express those wishes to medical personnel when you are unable to do so under circumstances described in your Living Will.

Heir: One who inherits property due to blood relationship.

Inactive Trust: A trust in which the trustee has no duty except to hold title to the property.

Inheritance Tax: A tax on the right to receive property by inheritance.

Insurance Trust: A trust fund that provides management of life insurance proceeds.

Intestate: *noun*, one who died without a valid will; *adjective*, having no valid will.

Irrevocable Trust: A trust which, by its terms, cannot be revoked (or can be changed or terminated only under certain conditions).

Marital Deduction Trust: Trust used to gain maximum benefit of the marital deduction by dividing property in half with a view toward having it escape taxation in the estate of the surviving spouse.

Pour-Over: A term referring to the transfer of property from an estate or trust upon the occurrence of an event as provided in the instrument.

Power of Attorney: A document authorizing an individual (or institution) to act as agent for another.

Probate: Method by which a will is proved to a court and accepted as valid.

The process by which an estate is administered and titles to a deceased person's assets are transferred.

Revocable Trust: A trust that can be revoked or changed at any time by the person who established it in the first place.

Testamentary Trust: A trust established by the provisions of a person's will for all or part of what that person leaves.

Trust: An agreement in which one person or institution (the trustee) is the holder of the legal title to property (the trust property) subject to a legally enforceable obligation to keep or use the property for the benefit of another (the beneficiary).

Trustee: An individual or trust institution that holds the legal title to property for the benefit of someone else.

Trust Estate: All the property in a particular trust account.

Will: A legally binding declaration of a person's wishes in writing regarding matters to be attended to after his death (usually relating to property) and inoperative until his death.

CHAPTER 5

Issues of the Heart

He listens, but he doesn't hear me. How can we communicate better?
My son finished college two years ago; he is still at home. What now?
Can I plan for the likelihood of caring for an aging parent?
Does stress really affect my health?
I recently divorced. How long will I feel this angry?

A t the heart of everything are relationships with loved ones. Whether those loved ones are family or friends, nothing is really as important. Nothing is as difficult, or rewarding, or grounding as how we live, love, work, play, and negotiate with those we care about. Our relationships often define us to others — Mary's husband, Juan's sister, Jack's new love interest. Yet we are a pretty diverse group in very diverse settings as mid-life approaches.

Some of us have been married 20 years or more with kids finishing school. Probably both partners work. Dual-career couples are more the norm than the exception. Half of us have been married and divorced. Many are single parents, heading households on our own. A growing segment of the population between 30 and 50 has never married. Or, you may be a blended family, bringing your offspring and your spouse's into the reconstituted and occasionally turbulent mix that most blended families experience.

As our lives change, our choices and challenges also change. This chapter explores some of the decisions that confront us in our 30s, 40s, and even our 50s as we pursue relationships in a variety of family structures.

Improving Relationships

In the work versus family struggle, partners must agree on priorities, and one priority must be the relationship. Knowing what the problems are in a relationship is not the same as knowing what to do about them. In his classic work, *Love and Will*, Rollo May describes the opposite of love as not hate, but apathy. Apathy does not foster security. Caring sensitivity to others is the exact opposite of indifference. An ever-present caring must be felt by those whom we love and those who need us.

Close, satisfying relationships are built by investing ourselves in others. It takes continuing effort to make "you and I" successfully into "we." The skills needed, however, are within everyone's reach and often are the same skills used in the workplace. Using these skills at home may require more time, thought, consideration, and patience because the relationships are more personal. Most families do not have policies in place to arbitrate disagreements and many family conflicts are unique. We are continually breaking new ground, and that can be challenging and rewarding, as well as irritating and exhausting.

Communication Styles

How we communicate not only affects discussions about money but can complicate all interaction between partners. Differences in style complicate understanding because issues are expressed differently. How do we express wants and needs? How do we feel about raising children? How do we feel about money? What are our priorities? Who makes these decisions? Understanding communication styles goes a long way toward reducing these tensions.

To express ourselves clearly, we must first know what it is we want to say. Men and women are raised and socialized differently. We all learn to ignore, express, or conceal different parts of ourselves. Over time this becomes habit and leads to the common complaint. We don't speak the same language. When a misunderstanding occurs, we search for reasons within each other's personalities. The problem lies not within persons, but in the communication between persons. Honest and effective communication often determines the quality of a relationship.

Communication is a learned process. It begins in childhood and continues throughout our lives. At or near the top of every survey on relationship satisfaction is good communication, including the following skills:

- Expressing thoughts, feelings, and preferences clearly
- Listening to and understanding the concerns of others
- Negotiating fairly and effectively to reach decisions jointly

Are we accurately interpreting what the other person has said? Often we begin to formulate our response before our partner has ceased to speak. By doing this, we miss valuable information and respond to only part of what they are saying, or to what we think they are going to say.

After you have listened fully, check your interpretation with your partner. In intimate relationships, it is important to check out not only the facts of the message, but also the feeling expressed, either verbally or nonverbally. Most of our misunderstandings come from our failure to check and make sure we have heard correctly. All of us have been in disagreements that end several minutes (or hours) later in puzzled agreement, only to discover there was never a difference of opinion, only a difference of language and understanding.

Flexible Attitudes

Relationship skills are as varied as the families within which they were developed. How did your family view the world? Was it a safe place, dangerous, good, or unpredictable? Were there feelings that were not allowed? Was conversation open or were there some subjects that were off limits? Were you, as a child, actively included in discussions? How we develop relationships, with whom, and how much we are willing to listen to others comes from the world view we have developed through our families and life experiences.

> *Experience is not what happens to a man, it is what a man does with what happens to him. It is a gift for dealing with the accidents of existence, not the accidents themselves.*
>
> Aldous Huxley

Remaining open and flexible in your attitudes can help in interpersonal relationships. Resist any tendencies to make judgments. Listen and try to understand the other's point of view. Challenge yourself to step beyond your assumptions or prejudices, and you will be rewarded with a richer world.

Self-Esteem — Mine and Yours

The ability to affirm others is rooted in how good we feel about ourselves. If we are realistic in our expectations of ourselves, then we are more likely to be affirming and supportive of others. We all have different skills and talents that develop in stages throughout our lifetime. Encouragement accepts the level of accomplishment that a person has reached and focuses on that effort. It means being more concerned that a person believe in himself than that he meet our particular expectations. It's separating any value judgments about a person from that person's actions, whether the judgments are positive or negative. In short, we need to learn to be accepting of ourselves and others as we are, not as we want to be, could have been, or wish we were.

Divorce: the Impact and the Alternatives

Separation brings a loss of the familiar, someone who was crucial to your identity. Whatever the quality of the marriage or the reasons for a divorce, it is always a difficult time. All relationships entail some risk, and although marriage involves a commitment, there are never any guarantees that the commitment will be permanent.

No one enters a marriage planning to divorce, but half of us do separate and divorce. Statistics show we are even less successful in maintaining second marriages. Few of us seek premarital counseling and our expectations may be unrealistic. Unsure of our expectations, we frequently do not communicate them and are both puzzled and hurt when our ideal is not met.

Research suggests that the behavior and attitudes of married couples is an indicator of the success of their marriage. While we can not yet predict divorce we are beginning to see what qualities lasting marriages have in common. Some of the findings are not what we might expect.

Couples who share a traditional interpretation of gender roles in a marriage are at less risk of divorcing than those who do not. Marriages that allow the couple individual autonomy and yet foster shared responsibility are also at low risk for divorce. However, couples whose relationship is characterized by cycles of fighting and sex, or those in which the wife raises problems and the husband dismisses them are both at higher risk of divorcing. Interestingly, case studies indicate that active listening is not as useful a technique as is learning to fight fair. Successful marriages are not those with fewer problems, but those with better problem-solving strategies. Couples who both worked to emphasize the positives in their partners while learning to accept a certain degree of imperfection were less likely to regard divorce as a solution to their relationship difficulties.

People are not perfect and neither are their marriages. Those marriages that survive, those we would call successful, seem to be between people who recognize that there is no such thing as a perfect relationship. They recognize and accept that ordinary people have to try extraordinarily hard to keep a relationship healthy and fulfilling.

A Period of Adjustment

Divorce can be devastating whether it occurs after two years or 20 years of marriage. If you or someone you know is going through a divorce, there are things you can do to help ease the pain, resentment and sense of abandonment that often accompanies divorce. The following chart lists some simple things we can do to help ourselves or others:

Divorcing Person	*As a Friend*
Ventilate. Bottling up feelings just prolongs them. Try to reconcile.	Be available. Ask them to talk. Listen. Hold the advice.
Allow your friends and family to listen and help.	Remain neutral. Focus on your friend's feelings and empathize with those.
Avoid blaming. The bitterness will drain you.	Highlight the positive aspects of your friend's life that will continue beyond the divorce.
Monitor your physical health. Eat and sleep regularly and maintain moderate exercise.	Socialize. Invite your friend to dinner and social gatherings.
Seek professional help. Counseling can be useful in a transition time such as divorce.	Offer information. The name of a good lawyer or counseling center may be very useful to your friend.
Give yourself time. Everyone responds and heals at their own rate.	Give them time. A divorce represents a major loss in a person's life. They may cycle through several series of anger, depression, and acceptance before it is resolved.

Divorcing spouses cycle through different stages, denial, anger, and depression, at varying stages and lengths of time. Healing and finding new direction will occur when the time is right for that person.

Focus and Negotiate

If you are divorced and considering remarriage, review the strategies discussed in this chapter. If you are married or remarried, make an appointment with your spouse to use these guidelines and give your marriage a checkup.

A study on the marital quality of dual-career couples found six variables crucial to increasing marital satisfaction and stability. Consider each variable independently, and rate your relationship on a scale of one to 10. Comparing your evaluations will show areas that might need improvement.

1. A satisfying social life — close family ties, outside friendships, community involvement — improves satisfaction in dual-career marriages.
2. A high level of positive regard (mutual respect) between spouses is another variable that increases marital stability when both parties work. This means couples perceive themselves as similar, attractive to one another, sharing similar values, and giving frequent support.
3. Couples with high-quality marriages perceive the benefits of two incomes as enhancing their lifestyle.
4. Marital satisfaction and stability increase when both partners are committed to the support of the wife's career.
5. Dividing tasks and discussing roles are also important to the development of marital satisfaction and stability. Most often husbands report a far higher level of household activity than their wives report for them.
6. Finally, marital satisfaction is enhanced when couples have frequent interaction and agreement on how to spend leisure time. Enjoying what you do together and sharing interests and values are vital to building and maintaining a satisfying relationship.

Finding Alternatives

Caryl S. Avery, a marriage therapist and writer, outlined eight steps to divorce-proof marriage:
1. Make your relationship a high priority.
2. Give it periodic checkups. Seek help when necessary. (It's necessary when either party feels it's necessary.)

3. Provide frequent support and encouragement. Avoid put-downs!
4. Aim for equality.
5. Keep lines of communication open. Remain non-judgmental and listen.
6. Keep in mind you must each like and respect yourself in the context of the relationship if it is to be truly meaningful.
7. Share joys as well as chores.
8. Make your marriage unique; don't compare. The grass is rarely greener in your friends' marriages. All marriages have problems.

Again, there are no guarantees, but knowing how to work at a marriage helps to reduce the risks. Marriage is not static. It's a process of often realigning expectations, commitments, and strategies. Evaluating what you feel, and why, can often strengthen your marriage.

Effective Parenting

Parenting presents additional challenges to our generation. We are already coping with dual careers, increased mobility, divorce, and remarriage. The strength of a family still appeals to most people contemplating marriage. We approach family issues and parenting with a mix of values and standards. Some are learned from our parents; others are created by our own life experiences. What we develop for our own families blends old traditions and new standards, molded to meet today's demands.

As parents, we must acknowledge the cumulative effects of less permanent lifestyles, changing social values, and increased use of day care. A child's view is altered by these personal, family, and societal changes. Parents, extended families, friends, day care centers, and preschools affect how children feel about themselves and the world around them. Through all these changes, as parents we want to provide a stable, nurturing environment for our children. We want the best for them. Following are basic principles that most people agree work well in rearing children.

A Structure of Love and Safety

Provide children with a caring environment based on a structure of love, direction, safety, and discipline. A caring environment is conducive to a child's sense of security. Their home is their haven for developing self-esteem and positive attitudes about the world around them. Anxieties, such as fear of abandonment, guilt, resentment, and frustration cause children to feel frightened and insecure.

A small child's greatest fear is of being unloved and abandoned. If separation is necessary, prepare your child with explanations. Tell him your destination and when you will return. Information usually reassures a child.

Praise should be given sincerely and appropriately. Praise should deal only with the child's efforts and accomplishments, not with his character or personality. Our words of praise should allow the child to draw his own realistic conclusions about his personality.

When a child's efforts are recognized and praised, the child will, most likely, attempt the next challenge. His safety is not threatened. If he tries and is ridiculed or ignored, he will hesitate or refuse to try the next time.

Consistency

Trust is very important in a child's life, and consistency teaches trust. Children need to know that some things in their changing lives will not change. Set guidelines for behavior, and enforce them consistently. A child's sense of security is jeopardized when a parent's responses are not consistent. Children need to know what is acceptable and unacceptable behavior.

Focus on the behavior, or the issue, not the child. This allows you a more constructive means to deal with the problem without damaging the child's self-esteem. Children raised with consistent and understood standards will learn to monitor themselves. They know when their behavior needs to be changed. Parental discipline that is positive, fair, firm, and consistent encourages self-discipline and self-reliance in children.

Think before you act. Find out the root cause of a child's behavior. Keep in mind the physical, the social, and the emotional needs of your child to determine what is motivating their behavior. Then select the appropriate course of action. Children test parents, and adults should not feel uneasy standing up to a misbehaving child.

Too often parents ignore inappropriate behavior in their children, resulting in those unwanted behavior patterns becoming established — bad habits. Don't be afraid to say no. This allows the child, if said in a calm, caring yet firm manner, to seek alternatives to accomplish his goals, wants, or needs.

Emotional Availability and Support

Nurturing the growth and development of your child demands your availability, particularly your emotional availability. Being there to give love and understanding provides the support for the variety of emotions children experience. A child's needs change, and being available to address these evolving feelings is critical to parenting well.

Parents are the source of information and shape a child's values through words and actions. Emotional availability suggests to your child that no matter how troublesome they may find a problem, you are concerned and ready to listen.

Talk to your children, and allow them to talk to you. Keep in mind their age, experiences, and frame of reference. Their logic is often short-term, driven by the need for immediate gratification. A parent who listens attentively conveys to the child that his ideas are valued. This respect for the child enhances the child's sense of self-esteem.

In the day-to-day pressures of work and family it's easy to minimize a child's concern. It is even easier to postpone a problem or question until a more convenient time. What is important to a child should not be prioritized by the parent. Take time, at that time, to listen, and give the support and encouragement needed.

Learning to Make Decisions

Rights, responsibilities, and privileges during childhood and teen years are, and always have been, a source of friction. When you give responsibilities to a child, you are training that child in decision making. Including your children in decisions, and allowing them some controlled choice, enhances their development as individuals. It also teaches them that they must live with the results of their choices. Expose children early to a system of ethics. Allow them to develop their own sense of right and wrong. Values cannot be taught directly. Children learn values by identifying with and imitating people who gain their love and respect. These values, assimilated at home and from the community, become part of the child. If a child lives with criticism, he learns to doubt his own judgment. He cannot learn responsibility if he is full of self-doubt.

Daily practice in exercising judgment and making choices appropriate to a child's age and understanding slowly develops responsibility. Select situations in which your child can make decisions, and then let the child make the choice. Some decisions fall entirely within the child's area of responsibility. There are decisions, however, that affect the child's welfare and are in the parent's area of responsibility. In such matters, the child may have a voice, but the parent makes the choice.

The Tougher Issues

Those of us who married and had children in our 20s are now the parents of adult children. Many of us have adult children who have remained or returned home. In addition many of us are also caring for aging parents. If you are caring for adult children and aging parents you are sandwiched between two areas of responsibility at a point in your life when freedom was what you expected. This affects your plans for the years ahead.

As women continue to delay childbearing into their 30s and 40s, and their parents live longer, increasing numbers will join the Sandwich Generation. They will have simultaneous responsibilities for both child and elder care. It is estimated that one of every four working adults in America is providing some form of support to a parent, older relative, or relative with a disability.

Although some men are taking more responsibility for dependent care, women remain the primary caregivers for both children and the elderly. Increases in the senior population predicted in the next decade mean that members of the Sandwich Generation will play a crucial role in the future of the American family.

Adult Children

Adult children remaining or returning home can extend the parent's role as caregiver. Although parenting is a lifetime pursuit, adult children remaining or returning home can affect activities, freedom, and financial goals of mid-career men and women. An increasing number of incompletely launched adults are returning home to live for a variety of reasons. Many college graduates today are moving back in with mom and dad to save money as they look for a job or pay off college loans. Unlike past generations, many young adults are delaying marriage and staying home into their late 20s and 30s.

Besides delayed marriage, higher education, and high cost of living, divorce is also sending adult children back home. Many marriages are ending in divorce, and divorce often causes an adult child (and even a grandchild) to need a place to live for awhile. Communication regarding roles and expectations is a must. Sit down together and discuss these issues, including financial and household responsibilities. The need for mutual respect should be understood. Simply put, treat adult children as adults.

Aging Parents

The New York-based Families and Work Institute reports that 40 percent of workers expect to be responsible for their aging parents in the next five years. According to sociologists, the care of aging parents in the U.S. is still being provided primarily by their own children. This affects your plans for the years ahead. This role reversal does not come naturally; we are all faced with becoming the caregiver for the person who took care of us all our lives. Such shifting roles are some of the harder aspects of dealing with aging parents.

As our parents struggle to maintain their independence, their needs become greater and, to their dismay, their dependency increases. We are caught between being the child, doing as we are told, and being the parent, doing what we think is best. Our role becomes that of a partner with our parents. As the situation evolves, and time takes its toll, our role may change from being a partner to being in control. Making difficult choices and heart-wrenching decisions can sometimes exhaust us both physically and emotionally and leave us facing financial issues involving family and caregiving decisions. Dealing with these issues is never easy. Try to maintain ongoing discussions with your parents and family members. Addressing these issues can help you, and your parents, plan for what lies ahead.

In our increasingly mobile society, the number of workers in their late 30s to mid-50s providing long-distance care for a family member is expected to double in the next 15 years. Public agencies and private firms are offering services to help elders and to relieve the burden on their caregivers. Assistance with personal chores, home delivered meals, and transportation is available free (or for a small voluntary contribution) to people 60 and over by local service agencies that receive federal funds. Many volunteer programs with visiting services and telephone check-in systems are also available free.

Relationships and Money

Family relationships and money form a strange mix of love, responsibility, active preparation, the acceptance of things you can't change, and wisdom that only comes with experience. It's learning and teaching, and, most of all, finding common ground with those you love. Nothing is more important.

Marriage and Remarriage

More than 50 percent of all marriages now end in divorce. With this in mind, more and more people consider a prenuptial agreement essential. There are three basic reasons for a prenuptial agreement:

1. To protect an estate for a previous spouse and/or children
2. To protect assets of the wealthier spouse in case of divorce
3. To set special financial conditions of the marriage

A prenuptial agreement can reduce family tension surrounding an anticipated second marriage. With such an agreement, neither family needs to worry about how that marriage will affect the inheritance of an estate. It also permits couples to accurately and fairly assess property and financial issues should the marriage dissolve.

Many states now set a minimum on the percentage of an estate a spouse must inherit. Consult a lawyer to ensure your prenuptial agreement is drafted to assure your wishes comply with the law and can be carried out.

There are several issues that should be included in any prenuptial agreement:
- Estate rights. Decide the minimum amount of assets to be bequeathed by each spouse to the other in event of death.
- Income, assets, and debts. Make a full disclosure of all income, assets owned, and debts owed.
- Assets. Decide which assets will be in your name, which assets will be in your spouse's name, and which assets will be held jointly.
- Divorce. Decide who will pay the bills for necessities — rent, mortgage, food, utilities, and luxuries. Decide about separate property assets, held before the marriage, and marital property assets, acquired during the marriage.
- Length. Decide on the length the agreement will remain valid (usually five to 10 years unless renewed).

A prenuptial agreement should be negotiated several months before marriage or remarriage. Each person involved should have his/her attorney and accountant, and each should pay his/her own legal fees. Establish your priorities — assets, lifestyle, property, children from previous marriages. Make sure you will be restored to your premarital state of living in the event of a divorce. Ask questions, and be sure you are aware of the divorce and inheritance laws in your state before you waive any rights. These are areas of potential conflict, and resolving them at the beginning leaves you and your partner free to concentrate on other aspects of the relationship.

Questions to Ask before Getting Married

What is your definition of commitment?
Have you discussed finances?
What about household responsibilities?
How close are you to family or friends?
How do you handle anger and other emotions?
How do you show love to each other?
How well did you discuss these very questions?

Blended Family Finances

Life happens! If you decide to blend your household and someone else's, life seems to happen faster and in more unexpected ways. There are many challenges because you did things one way, and now other ways must be considered. Seek common ground and compromise. Realize early where the potential volatile issues lie, and attempt to address them before combining families. One problem area may be finances. Everyone brings baggage, and sometimes that baggage includes how money, or the lack of it, may have been used in the past as a tool to build, destroy, or hold hostage a relationship.

Of all the icy blasts that blow on love, a request for money is the most chilling and havoc-wreaking.

Gustave Flaubert

More marriages end over money issues than any other cause. Take seriously the need to build a way to successfully communicate about finances. Not talking about it, assuming you're "already on the same page" only invites disaster. Too much discussion, without first listening for a clearer understanding of your partner's views, will only build resentment and ultimately payback.

Mastering the Possibilities

Here are a few areas that are ripe for misunderstanding and conflict. Take some time to think about your values and your goals when reviewing these. Blended families and blending finances is not a science with hard and fast rules; it's an art . . . the art of the possible.

Who handles the finances in our household? The person who is the best at handling finances should be the one doing it, with one caveat — full disclosure regarding everything you do. In most relationships, one party will have more experience and expertise in money management. When one person has the dominant role in financial matters, however, key issues need to be discussed fully. These issues should include, but not be limited to:

- Living within a weekly/monthly budget
- Establishing a budget together, monitoring it for areas that need improvement, and modifying it when appropriate
- Determining how often and who will pay household bills and establishing a routine for doing that
- Prioritizing and separating what goes into the common pot for household expenses and what expenses will be covered by individual accounts
- Staying honest with each other with regard to spending and saving patterns

What's Your Priority?

Everyone is different, but some essentials require immediate attention — the mortgage, utilities, car payments, day care, etc. When those expenses are covered, and covered in a timely fashion, the challenge of prioritizing or "spending what's left" begins. For many of us, there isn't anything left!

If you do have discretionary, or left-over money, find a quiet time and place to discuss if or how to spend it. List three or four high-priority items, and then list the positives and negatives of each. This gives you a way to determine which of your priorities has the largest number of advantages. Look particularly for long-term financial advantages. That is probably the one deserving the most serious consideration.

Of course, things aren't always easy. Many times you'll find that all your priorities are "Class A" priorities, deserving attention, and you just can't decide. Or maybe each time the two of you sit down to discuss this, it seems that you reach an immediate impasse. If that's the case, don't hesitate to seek outside help. You may have very different communication styles or differing priorities. These problems are best addressed by a family therapist.

If you simply need advice on money management and competing priorities, you may want to talk with a *Consumer Credit Counseling Service* representative. This nonprofit organization can help with those decisions.

My Money, Your Money, and Our Money

Conventional wisdom suggests that, at least initially, a joint account should be used to pay for all shared expenses. These would include a mortgage, utilities, food, clothing, day care, outstanding expenses, etc. If both of you work, using a jointly funded account for these common items makes sense. This account pays for the high-priority bills. In addition, each of us has personal wants. These items should be funded by your separate personal account. That way, funds in the joint account aren't spent on personal items before the family essentials are covered.

This three-account system may not be necessary once you've successfully blended your financial lives. It is, however, a relatively easy and efficient way to set up a family financial management system in the early stages.

Aging Parents and Money

This is a tougher issue to deal with than that of an irresponsible adult child. Here all the psychological trappings of a parent/child relationship are present. Your parent is always your parent! That said, once in a while you may have to take responsibility for the finances of an aging parent who acted unwisely or imprudently. This issue geometrically compounds in complexity when multiple siblings with multiple ideas on what's best for Mom enter the fray.

At some point, most people will assist an aging relative with finances. These transfers in financial responsibility are natural. If your parent is lucky enough to live a long life, you will undoubtedly need to first assist and perhaps later take full responsibility. If, however, an aging relative is acting irresponsibly, the shift of responsibility takes on an entirely different purpose and plan. You may need to protect that aging relative from themselves. To do this, you'll need to take some control. This is not an easy task, especially if you can't reach a consensus with other family members regarding the direction you should collectively take.

Let's assume, for the sake of this example, that consensus among siblings has been achieved. What, then, are your options? You or another family member could, with permission, take over control of the aging parent's finances. Then you or someone else would be responsible for paying bills, providing an income stream to your aging relative, and serving as both judge and jury on most financial decisions. Taking control is truly a thankless job. A less personal alternative is to set up a trust account. Trusts don't die as do family members. They are not bombarded with the psychological and emotional pressure of an aging relative's care. Establishing a trust may be costly, but it can reduce the friction inherent in taking over an aging parent's finances.

A third alternative is to take all or a portion of your parent's funds and purchase an annuity. An annuity contract is a financial product with insurance companies. This product does a couple of things quite well. The annuity contract is funded, often with a lump sum; you then may wish to annuitize or activate it. Once an aging parent begins receiving income distribution, that distribution is set. It provides a monthly income for life or for an aging person's life with a survivor benefit. Annuities have many options. The money is locked in place with the purpose of providing a monthly income stream. Family members can't tap into it, normally. As long as the annuitant lives, the income stream (monthly check) comes until their death. Any money remaining will be guided by whoever the annuitant's survivor is or by the laws of descent and distribution in your state. What have you accomplished with an annuity? You've collectively decided to take funds out of the hands of an aging parent and to put those funds into an annuity that will provide a monthly income stream.

Deferred annuities are one of the many tax-deferred retirement investments. As with an IRA or 401k, you don't pay any taxes until you begin making withdrawals. When you decide to withdraw the money (typically at age 59½), you have several distribution choices. Deferred annuities come in two flavors, *fixed* or *variable*. Variable annuities are popular because you have a variety of options. In difficult stock markets, people seeking shelter and predictability find a fixed annuity appealing. What's more, there is a floor on a fixed annuity that guarantees it won't provide less than a certain interest rate, typically 3 percent.

Teenagers and Money

You may not owe your kids a car when they turn 16; you may not owe them a college education; you may not even owe them an allowance. But you do owe your kids an education about money. To get you started, here are some lessons every teenager should learn before they head out on their own.

There are times when parenthood seems nothing but feeding the mouth that bites you.

Peter DeVries

- Debt stinks! It's wise to establish credit, and most of us still need one or two credit cards, but use credit sparingly.
- Pay yourself first. No, that doesn't mean buying an iPod; it means a savings account to keep you out of debt.
- Watch out for the small stuff. A $3.25 cup of espresso each morning is $845 a year. Invested that can grow into a sizable amount over five or 10 years.
- Invest in a market index. To reach your long-term goals, you need the power of the stock market. With index investing, it's simple to get market-matching returns that, over time, could make you financially secure.
- Start a Roth IRA as soon as you start earning money.
- Budgets are good. Track your income and expenses.
- Keeping up with the Joneses is a loser's game. Don't let the glitter fool you. Develop a plan and stick to it.
- Don't trust your money to anyone. Your money is your responsibility.
- Money can't buy happiness or love, but it can help you avoid misery.

Choices and Challenges

I feel my career has plateaued. What can I do?
How can I better balance my family and my work?
How can I develop a career plan that works?
With all this downsizing, how can I look out for myself?
Will it hurt my career to be a political spectator, not a player?

Today's workplace is more demanding and far more turbulent than in past decades. A large, well-qualified, fiercely competitive peer population means our working life will take on new dimensions. The oldest baby boomers are now in their 60s, the youngest in their early 40s. Upward career mobility is no longer readily available to everyone. The expectations of this generation are often so high that they outrun the available opportunities. The accelerating rate of change means more frequent career crises.

Nothing stays the same for long! Preparing for change by managing the resources and talent you have can mean the difference between success and failure. The most important message for all workers is that career advancement is in your hands. The age of career entitlement is gone forever. Take control of your own destiny and career.

Reinventing Your Career

Change is one of the few constants in today's workplace. Employees are facing changing mandates, budget constraints, and mixed messages as organizations downsize, merge, and reestablish their core business strategies. According to the American Management Association, of 259 Fortune

500 senior executives interviewed, 84 percent said their organizations had at least one major business transformation in the works.

Your job, and the jobs of thousands of others, will be to get more done with less. You will make career changes within your field and more of you will plateau earlier than in the past. These frustrations will cause many of you to reassess your career choices. Training, retraining, and embracing new skills will be more important. Your skills come from your abilities and experience; sharpen them and keep them portable.

You can expect the new transient quality of the workforce to persist. The dynamics that kept people working a lifetime for one company are shifting. Your career advancement is in your hands, but you may need to adjust your attitude. Company loyalty may be less important than adaptability.

Those in their 30s and 40s have far-reaching work expectations, but 80% of baby boomers said that they would continue working in some way once they were "retired." Of this group, 23 percent said they expect to work part-time because they will need the income. That will create a lot of roadblocks for career mobility. Because of that potential, more companies and federal and state governments are developing "phased retirement" programs for older workers who want to ease into retirement not jump into it.

Work and worth form an intimate connection throughout our lives. Work helps us define who we are. It is often as important as family in how we feel about ourselves. Nurtured on prosperity and the value of higher education, this generation expects to move into careers providing personal fulfillment, lots of money, and professional growth. Not everyone gets a piece of that pie, and the ego/work connection suffers. The unlimited vistas you thought were available when you began your career narrow with more competition, fewer positions, and maturity. Doing what you like, doing something that holds meaning, something of worth, is still important and should be pursued.

Job satisfaction is based on knowing what you want to do, and then doing it. Some workers find themselves trapped in jobs they don't like. They may receive excellent compensation, but eventually the intangible issues — lack of challenge, too little responsibility, and vague career direction — will take their toll. If you're unhappy at work, all aspects of your life suffer. You won't be able to compete effectively with those who love their work.

At home, this dissatisfaction can affect how you see yourself and how you relate to your family. Job dissatisfaction always increases the potential of burnout.

Adapting to a Changing Workplace

Workplace cultures, built over a period of years, change overnight, and any employee can be affected. Commit yourself to working through and adjusting to reorganizations. Adapting to change requires positioning yourself for minimal damage and maximum opportunity. More of us will work in teams or on a temporary or project basis. Plan to be a part of the change. Cultivate perspectives that accommodate the uncertainty any change brings. You must have a willingness to change if you hope to move your career forward.

New technologies require an understanding of the dynamics, opportunities, and impact of that technology on product and process. Awareness of the impact of technology on markets, organizations, and people is knowledge that can only aid in career competition. Gaining this new training is neither easy nor cheap. It is important, however, for it drives the accelerating rate of change in America. Here are some positive ideas for adapting:

- Reinvent your job. Become the department expert on the new computer system, and you may see your duties shift agreeably. Take a fresh look at your situation/options. Don't be limited by your job description.
- Get involved in coordinating volunteer efforts for your company. Eventually, you may find such short-term projects evolve into new jobs within your organization. Seek out assignments that you feel suit your needs and talents.
- Work from home; telecommute. If your dissatisfaction lies not in your job but in the time away from home, ask your supervisor if you could work from home. You save commuting time and may find you have more energy for both your job and family. Working from home is not an easy option suited to everyone or every job. Do your homework and plan carefully before you make any decisions.
- Go back to school. Many companies offer seminars, short courses, or other support for employees who want to pursue further education. Such opportunities sharpen your skills, keep you at the top of your field, or may facilitate a move into a new area.

- Treat your organization as your client. You may want to see yourself as a contractor selling your services to your employer. Be professional, but keep your own best interests at heart. The bottom line? An entrepreneurial spirit is an asset in today's workplace. As a motivated, self-directed worker, your professionalism and expertise may surpass those of the traditional 30-year employee.

Career Plateauing

With the dawn of a new century, many of us have found our careers have plateaued. The fast track upward has flattened out. Plateauing is not new, but it occurs earlier than it has for previous generations. In our parents' generation, plateauing often took place in one's 50s. At that time, many people felt, with retirement on the horizon, pushing for the next promotion was neither personally nor professionally worthwhile. Now, with people plateauing as early as their late 30s, the issue is a concern to both employees and employers. Employees beginning to feel the vague discomfort of a career possibly plateaued must realize part of the reason is that others have similar, or greater, or more diverse talents and similar aspirations.

Executive Congestion

If intense competition has brought earlier plateauing, then plateauing in general occurs because of the traditional organizational structure of American businesses and government agencies. As employees move up in the organization, the number of available key positions decreases and that stimulates executive congestion. Not everyone, however, ascends to upper level positions. Competing effectively means you'll need not only perseverance and creativity, but also access to information others may not have, along with political savvy and, of course, luck.

Redefining Success

The concept of plateauing is actually a by-product of our culture and our definition of success. For many, career success is measured primarily by promotions, more money, more responsibility, and the perks that come with advancement. If advancement doesn't come, we may see ourselves as less successful, passed over, or dead-ended. Both employers and employees must acknowledge plateauing and address the problems that it causes. What is needed is a redefinition of what determines success in a changing workforce. Both employers and employees must contribute to that redefinition.

Three Forms of Plateauing

In her book *The Plateauing Trap*, Judith M. Bardwick describes three forms of career plateauing. The first is **structural plateauing**. The hierarchical structure of most organizations can lead to career stagnation. Opportunities for advancement decrease as a competitive workforce scrambles for position.

The second form is **content plateauing**. Many employees who are structurally plateaued, which is essentially inescapable, are also content plateaued. Content plateauing begins when people know their jobs too well; there are not enough new challenges. Job excitement has decreased, and their job has become routine.

The third form is **life plateauing**. When work becomes the most significant factor in a person's life, it is the basis of their identity and self-esteem. If promotions end, there is a sense of failure. Mastery of their work also brings feelings of boredom. People who feel plateaued in life usually feel trapped; they don't know how to break out of the cycle of despair, and they are afraid to try.

The fact is that everyone plateaus. People who feel plateaued want to experience their work and their lives differently. The first step is gaining insight — continuing to learn and be productive at work and continuing to mature and change in your life. Accepting that you are plateaued means recognizing that you're at the end of a phase, and then you are in a position to begin a new one.

Assessing Skills and Defining Goals

There is a difference between a career and a job. Careers are usually built and carefully cultivated. Jobs are less carefully selected and, consequently, less meaningful. Career planning is active, not reactive. It's a continuous process of deciding how, when, and where steps are to be taken. Planning leads to action; this should lead to achieving goals.

You cannot decide where you want to go without first determining where you are and where you've been. You acquire, expand, and modify your skills by every project you undertake. Increased skills can mean new directions and new goals. Understanding your worth and potential enhances your ability to realistically define new career goals and select the appropriate strategies to achieve them.

Career planning has four basic steps.

1. Assessing your past experiences
2. Evaluating your present position
3. Defining your career goals
4. Developing strategies to achieve those goals

Step 1: Assessing Your Past Experiences

Inventory the skills you possess, both professional and personal, what you have learned from previous jobs, and your accomplishments. Your past plays a significant role in how you approach career planning. The skill categories listed in Step 2 are areas in which you may have experience. Some relate to your profession while others represent skills you may have learned through parenting, professional seminars, continuing education courses, or leisure activities. The skills you have built over the past five, 10, or 15 years are transferable. Career planning can be approached through this transfer of skills.

Step 2: Evaluating Your Present Position

Look at your experiences and the skills you have built over the years. Examine your present career goals. How can these be updated, or modified, to enhance your future? Jobs revolve around managing people, data, and things. Technical skills, analytical skills, and communication skills are learned proficiencies. Analyze your present work skills to evaluate what you bring to your career now and what you might bring in the future.

Think about your current skills in the following categories. In which areas do you have strengths? Which areas do you need to concentrate on in the future?

Communicating. Written and oral communication is an integral part of your job. You are involved in presentations, group discussions, preparing, editing, and evaluating written reports, etc.

Problem Solving and Decision Making. Your job requires identifying problems, obtaining usable and applicable information, making decisions.

Planning/Organizing. In your job, you set goals, forecast trends, organize time.

Controlling/Delegating. You routinely monitor and evaluate the performance of others, define/carry out policy regarding people, responsibilities, and work flow.

Leading/Staffing. You're involved with hiring, training, terminating subordinates, maximizing performance toward organizational goals.

Functional/Technical. You are concerned with the practical understanding of programs or groups affecting your performance in your field.

Scheduling/Budgeting. Your job requires you to set, justify, and adhere to goals and targets for yourself and the organization.

List examples from your current job and you have the basis for a practical approach to marketing your skills in terms any employer can understand. This exercise provides only a track to run on. It's up to you to refine how to market your specific talents. Looking at each job or position in terms of the skills it requires or the skills it can teach is the essence of career planning. Each position should be a learning experience, building and expanding on the previous one.

Step 3: Defining Your Career Goals

Consider your present goals and objectives. What do you seek in a career? Do you want great financial reward? Do you need only a means to keep you busy? Do you seek challenge? What do l want is the most important question you can ask, but it is often the most difficult to answer. Define both short-term and long-range plans. Attainable goals are written in clear, precise terms. Many people long for better jobs; others simply put in their time, retired on active duty.

Action taken in career planning is calculated movement, and the movements you make often involve risk. Little is ever achieved, however, without risk. Planning and tracking your movements in pursuit of new careers is essential. Assess the risk associated with the actions you take, and develop contingency plans. List any obstacles you foresee that might hinder your accomplishing your career goals. Set goals, anticipate change, and build alternative strategies to reach your objective.

List three career goals for each of the following time frames. These goals should be achievable, challenging, measurable, and they should be dated.

Six month goals	Target date	Date achieved

One year goals	Target date	Date achieved

Three year goals	Target date	Date achieved

Step 4: Strategies — How to Get There!

Once you know your abilities and your goals, you must select effective strategies to reach your career and life objectives. Any strategy that is effective must also be flexible to accommodate the adjustments you will make along the way. The average American works for 10 different employers in his or her lifetime. Most spend only three-and-a-half years in one position before changing jobs. You'll change jobs more frequently than your parents did. Personal choice and professional demands are the main catalysts to career movement.

Career Planning Strategies

When you begin a job, there is a period of enthusiasm, interest, and exploration. This honeymoon may last months or even a year. When it's over, you may feel disillusioned. Throughout the job life cycle, there will be times of renewed interest that come with increased job experience. At some point, however, you or your employer will feel it's time for you to move up — to be promoted.

Moving Up

When you work for an agency or company, you like to feel you can work within that organization to move your career forward. Most Fortune 500 companies have implemented succession planning for top professionals. Management has the quasi-responsibility to assist you in not only developing career alternatives but also in acknowledging that if you're ambitious and a valued employee, you'll be rewarded. It's a two-way street. You have to reaffirm your value to the organization, and the organization must provide movement for your career goals.

> *A ship in the harbor is safe, but that is not what ships are built for.*
> John A. Shedd

Almost everyone wants upward mobility. You assume there's more status, more income, more challenge. Culturally, if you move up, it's assumed you're successful and valued. Everyone wants to be valued, but upward mobility has its risks, and timing is critical to successfully moving up in your career. Growing within an organization has advantages over seeking outside job opportunities. You are in an environment you know. You are aware of the positives and negatives. It's secure. There are other advantages, such as accrued pension and profit sharing, insurance plans, etc. These security factors, however, may not be as important as job satisfaction, growth, challenge, independence, and responsibility. The decision whether to remain in a job you know and are comfortable with or to take on something new is always difficult. Finances, emotional makeup, circumstances and, most of all, what you want for the future, all affect your decision.

Lateral Mobility

You may assume career mobility means upward mobility. Wiser career strategists, however, realize that careers can also move laterally. Every career step does not have to be a step up. Lateral moves can provide new challenges and different perspectives and experiences that broaden you for later career advancement. In the past, when organizations were less geared to specialty areas, lateral movement was common. It rounded out employees, familiarizing them with different facets of the organization. The more you know about how different business components work together, the greater will be your worth to your employer. Choosing a lateral move suggests flexibility and little fear of change, attributes that are valued by upper management.

Politics and the Organization: Spectator or Player

Politics is part of every organization, and it's subjective in nature. You must decide whether to participate or watch. Politics is the art of gaining and retaining power. Once you gain power, using that power is defined as tactics. Politics and power turn many people off. You like to believe hard work will be recognized and will move your career forward. This does not always happen. Politics and power have a role, and it's important to acknowledge that. Power can mean the ability to be effective, influential, and instrumental in implementing change. The positive and pragmatic reasons for gaining power can serve you well. Power is composed of three parts.

The first part is the position itself and what's implied in the position's authority. The second is how you are perceived by the group your power influences and how it limits, or expands, your abilities to lead. Finally, power rests with you and how you exercise your choices. Successfully gaining and retaining power incorporates several techniques:

Mentoring. Mentoring is affiliating with an individual or individuals in positions of power who advise you and aid your career and professional advancement. As they move up the organization, you will too. This technique, along with networking, has become an increasingly important tactic for career mobility.

Building Alliances. In any organization, some individuals fast-track. Some people will be promoted earlier, stand out, and shine more brightly. Build alliances with those in more powerful, more responsible, and more mobile positions. Be aware of organizational dynamics and needs, then try to grow into those needs.

Communication. One of the major causes of career stagnation is ineffectively communicating your career aspirations. Don't keep quiet! Identify those people who can help. Many times they will have critical, and frequently confidential, information that can aid you in managing career politics more effectively. Seek out informal channels of communication and know when to limit the information you're providing.

Selling Yourself Online

How people find work has changed. One change involves employers using the web to recruit and screen potential employees. It redefines how we seek employment. Now much of the initial work can, and should, be done electronically. Andy Grove, chairman of Intel, said, "Digital resumes, digital employment advertising, digital resume searches — it's rebuilding the infra-structure of job search." Business has gravitated quite quickly to web hiring. The web may be the recruiting tool of choice for many companies, dramatically decreasing the cost of hiring. By reducing recruitment costs and broadening the applicant pool, employers hire more efficiently or, at least, narrow the field of qualified applicants. Employers can quickly tap into a global applicant pool, screen by key word, and then, perhaps, test applicants in web-based testing sessions. Background checks can be done online and video-link software makes it easy to conduct initial candidate interviews.

Resumes. You did the resume. You sent out letters of inquiry. Maybe you had a reply, more likely, you didn't. The cycle continues — more resumes, more letters. The system doesn't always work for people seeking career change. Does this mean that the old tools don't work? No, it only means that there are new tools to use with the best of the old tools — effective networking strategies, strong interviewing skills, and timely follow-up.

Key Words . . . Key Phrases. If you don't have them, your resume won't be read. If it's not read, you're out. Next question! Stick with nouns when doing your web resume. Nouns show up in key word searches. Resume databases list skills — specific software skills, data processing knowledge, foreign languages, personnel experience, equipment proficiency, etc. Be specific, name names.

Don't Stop with One Resume. Everyone is multifaceted. Break down and classify your abilities. Most people can easily come up with two or three different skill sets. For instance, you may have managed a team, trained them, and been responsible for managing their budget. Three resumes can come from that one position — one for team building/management, one for training/employee development, and one for budgeting.

Searching Online. Make several tries at designing industry-specific resumes. When your efforts please you, you're ready to begin your web search. Fortune magazine reported that two-and-a-half million people had posted their resumes on the Internet. Almost 30,000 websites offer job-posting services. Should you post your resume on a large site like **monster.com** or a smaller, more industry-specific site? Increase your odds. Do both! Don't over generalize. Remember, industry-specific key words and key phrases get electronic attention, and that's what you want. A huge job site like monster.com or careermosiac.com may get many hits, but using industry-, skill-, or even company-specific sites can improve your search effectiveness.

Using a web search engine, you can search for jobs or specific industry position availability. The original search results will be pages and pages of sites. Use the search engine's capabilities to limit and target your search by searching within the original results or narrowing your search request to fit your needs.

Most search engines are capable of advanced search techniques and it is worth taking the time to understand how to increase the accuracy of your searches by using the operators supported by the site. Explanations on how to conduct an advanced search are readily available and easily understood.

Social Security and Pensions

Is my pension plan protected?
With all the politics, how might Social Security change?
Will I need additional health insurance to supplement Medicare?
How are my benefits affected if I return to work?
What happens to my tax-deferred savings plan if I change jobs?

E mployees today change careers more frequently than did previous generations. Increasing numbers of employees work part-time during their career or after they retire. These trends can affect future benefits. It's very important to understand where the money will come from to achieve your retirement goals. People usually have three income sources in retirement:

- Pension,
- Social Security, and
- Investment income or savings

Social Security

At retirement, a sizable portion of your income may come from Social Security. However, Social Security was not intended to be your only source of income. It is meant to supplement your pension, investment income, and savings. It is estimated that 95 percent of all workers are covered by Social Security, yet many of us do not understand how the system works. Many people think Uncle Sam takes money out of your paycheck, saves it for you, and pays it to you in the form of a monthly Social Security benefit check when you retire. Social Security doesn't work like that!

Social Security is an income transfer program. Payments to participate in Social Security are called FICA taxes, named after the Federal Insurance Contributions Act. Each year you pay a percentage of your wages to participate in the program. A limit is set on the total FICA taxes paid each year. Employers pay a matching amount. Your Social Security deductions, and those of other workers, are funding the benefits of today's retirees. When you retire, your benefits will be paid by all those still working. Each generation of workers, therefore, funds a generation of retirees. It is a pay-as-you-go system that has changed dramatically since the first Social Security benefits were paid out in 1941.

Maximum Annual Taxable Earnings

FICA payroll taxes are paid on all earnings up to the taxable wage base. This taxable wage base changes annually. The 1.45 percent of the 7.65 percent that comes out of your paycheck is paid on all earned income. There is no taxable wage base for the Medicare tax. If you earn a million dollars, 1.45 percent will be paid to Medicare. The following chart shows Social Security taxable wage bases and payroll tax rates.

	FICA Payroll Tax*		*Medicare Payroll Tax*	
Year	**Wage Base**	**FICA Rate**	**Wage Base**	**Medicare Rate**
2012	$110,100	4.20%	all wages	1.45%
2011	$106,800	4.20%	all wages	1.45%
2010	$106,800	6.20%	all wages	1.45%
2009	$106,800.00	6.20%	all wages	1.45%
2008	$102,00.00	6.20%	all wages	1.45%

* Workers pay tax on income up to the wage base. In 2011, the employee share of payroll taxes draopped to 4.2%. This is only for 2012, the tax returns to 6.2% in 2013 unless Congress votes to retain 4.2%. Unlikely!

Earnings Estimate

Your Social Security benefit is based on age and the amount of earnings reported for you over your entire working career. When you receive your paycheck, do you know how the payroll taxes were computed? Do you know what earnings and work years have been reported for you? The Social Security Administration now has an online Personalized Earnings and Benefits Estimate for all working Americans, age 25 or over. Access your statement 90 days before your birth month. At ssa.gov, review the information carefully and report any errors to the Social Security Administration at 1-800-772-1213.

You can also access the Social Security website to request an estimate of your future benefits, apply for a new or replacement card, get information on benefits programs, check cost-of-living adjustments (COLAs) and current earnings limitations, and request an additional Statement of Earnings. Since wage index factors and national average wages change yearly, it's best to inquire before relying on any estimated benefit. If you have questions about your Social Security benefit, contact your nearest Social Security office.

Computing Your Benefits

When your benefits are computed, actual earnings for past years are adjusted to take into account the changes in average wages since 1951. Your adjusted earnings are then averaged together, and a formula is applied to the average to get your benefit rate. This ensures that your benefits reflect the changes in your wages over your entire career. Before you retire, visit your local Social Security office to discuss more personal questions with a representative.

Quarters of Coverage

Before any benefits can be paid to you or your family, you need a certain number of quarters of coverage, or credits for work under Social Security. A quarter of coverage is used to determine the amount of work you have. In 2012, you receive one quarter of coverage for each $1,130 earned. Each year that figure increases, and you cannot earn more than four quarters per year. Those born in 1929 or later need 40 quarters of coverage to be eligible for retirement benefits. That equals working under Social Security, paying into the system, for 10 years.

Applying for Benefits

It is usually recommended that you apply for Social Security benefits 60 to 90 days before you retire. If you retire before age 62, wait until approximately three months before your 62nd birthday to apply. Age 62 is the earliest a worker can receive benefits, and at age 62 benefits are reduced. The reduction percent depends on your birth date. Unreduced benefits are paid if you begin benefits at your full retirement age. If you work past your full retirement age, delaying benefits, you will receive an additional 8 percent for each year beyond your full retirement age up to the age of 70.

Many people opt to take reduced Social Security benefits at age 62, before reaching their full retirement age. It often takes several years to make up the difference between your age-62 benefits and the benefit you would earn by waiting until your full retirement age. If you have earned 40 credits, you can start receiving Social Security benefits at age 62 or at any time between age 62 and your full retirement age. However, your benefits will be permanently reduced based on the number of months you receive benefits before you reach your full retirement age.

For example, if your full retirement age is 67 and you begin receiving benefits at age 62, your benefits will be reduced by 30 percent. If you begin receiving benefits at age 63, your benefits will be reduced by 24 percent. If you wait until age 64 to begin receiving benefits, your benefit will be reduced by 18 percent.

Social Security Reduced Benefits/Delayed Retirement

Birth Date	Full Retirement Age	% of Benefit at age 62	Delayed Retirement Credit
1937 & earlier	65	80.00%	6.5%*
1938	65 and 2 months	79.17%	6.5%
1939	65 and 4 months	78.33%	7.0%
1940	65 and 6 months	77.50%	7.0%
1941	65 and 8 months	76.67%	7.5%
1942	65 and 10 months	75.83%	7.5%
1943-54	66	75.00%	8.0%
1955	66 and 2 months	74.16%	8.0%
1956	66 and 4 months	73.34%	8.0%
1957	66 and 6 months	72.50%	8.0%
1958	66 and 8 months	71.67%	8.0%
1959	66 and 10 months	70.83%	8.0%
1960 & later	67	70.00%	8.0%

The delayed retirement credit is the percentage of increase in your benefits if you delay receiving any benefits until beyond your full retirement age.

Earnings Limitations

Each year Social Security establishes limits on how much you can earn and still receive full benefits. You don't have to stop working totally to receive Social Security benefits, but if you earn more than the earnings limit, and you are under your full retirement age, your Social Security benefits will be reduced by one dollar for every two dollars you earn above the limit. Earnings do not include pension amounts, investment income, interest, Social Security and veteran's benefits, trust fund income, annuities, capital gains, gifts or inheritances, moving and travel expense reimbursements, jury duty pay, and certain sick pay and realty income. The earnings limit for 2012 is $1,220 a month or $14,640 a year.

Earnings Limit

Age	2012	
	Monthly	**Yearly**
65	$1,220	$14,640
66+	no limit	no limit

Source: ssa.gov

If you continue to work after receiving benefits, you will continue to pay taxes on your earnings. What you pay is, of course, based on your income. However, working after you begin receiving benefits could raise your benefit amount later on. Your benefits would then be automatically recomputed by Social Security.

Medicare Coverage

Medicare coverage is not always complete health care coverage. Medicare has two parts: Part A (Hospital Insurance) and Part B (Supplementary Medical Insurance). Part B is optional coverage, and you must pay a monthly premium. The premium in 2012 is $99.90. Home health care is being phased into Part B coverage. The deductible amount is $140. Medicare becomes available at age 65 even if you're still employed.

If you are single (file an individual tax return) and your yearly income is more than $85,000, or if you are married (file a joint tax return) and your income is more than $170,000, your Part B monthly premiums will be more costly. This is called "means testing" and it imposes much higher costs on high-income earners. Medicare has established "a beachhead" for means testing your benefits. This could easily be implemented by Social Security as it struggles to address more retirees and less revenue in the future.

If you are between 65 and 69 and are covered by your employer's group health plan, certain provisions will apply to your receiving Medicare. If you continue working past age 65, you must apply for Medicare with the Social Security office; otherwise your application will not be processed until you apply for Social Security retirement benefits.

Medicare now offers insurance coverage for prescription drugs through Medicare Part D for traditional fee-for-service coverage (Medicare Parts A and B) or through one of the Medicare Advantage plans (HMO, PPO, etc.). After the $310 deductible is met, Medicare Part D will pay 75 percent of drug costs up to $2,930 per year. vEnrollees pay 100 percent of the drug costs between $2831 and $6,440, and then Medicare reimburses 95 percent of costs above $6,440. Individuals who are not eligible for prescription drug coverage through their retiree medical, or who have company retiree drug benefits that are less comprehensive than Medicare Part D, should consider enrolling in Part D. If your drug coverage is at least as good as that offered by Medicare, you do not need to enroll in Part D.

Taxes on Social Security

When you begin receiving benefits, those benefits can be taxed. If you are single and your income in retirement, from all income sources, exceeds $34,000, then 85 percent of your Social Security benefit is taxable as ordinary income. If you are married, the income threshold is $44,000. Income sources include almost everything—pension, Social Security benefits, investment income, rental property income, etc.

The Future of Social Security

The clock is ticking for Social Security. The system Franklin Roosevelt grandly established in 1935 is approaching its 80th birthday. Now a huge group of baby boomers is ready for retirement benefits. In survey after survey, workers under 45 doubt the ability of the system to provide them with benefits equivalent to their contributions. Can the system deliver and deliver for the long haul? That's the question.

When Congress does act, the solution will likely be a combination of elements under discussion. In addition to efforts to increase the amount of money available, changes may include some combination of increased payroll taxes, decreased benefits, and an increased age at which workers become eligible for benefits.

Each year the trustees of both the Social Security system and Medicare update their projections on the health and solvency of the two systems. In 2011, the trustees estimated that Social Security would stay solvent until 2017. They were wrong! Social Security is projected to run a deficit from now on. Six years before the trustees expected it to happen. Medicare trustees state that the hospital insurance trust fund financed by payroll taxes will be exhausted by 2019. However, the insolvency projections keep fluctuating depending on the economic assumptions used in the calculation more/less economic growth, higher/lower interest rates, higher/lower inflation, higher/lower hospital costs, and rising/falling unemployment.

Social Security is still a political football. The chair of the Federal Reserve has said that either taxes will have to increase, the retirement age will have to be raised, or the benefits of future retirees will have to be decreased. His directness, while unpopular, lays out the limited choices facing Congress and the President.

Over the next two years, Social Security will change, but it will not change for everyone. Older employees will, in all likelihood remain in the existing system. Younger employees will become part of a revised system. Since Social Security is currently the most important income source for retirees (40 percent of all income received by those over age 65) wise planners should investigate alternative funding strategies. Social Security and Medicare may ultimately remain solvent much longer than expected but no one can afford to bet the quality of their retirement on that expectation. Hope for the best but plan for the worst.

Pension Plan Basics

Your pension will probably provide the largest part, but not the only part, of your retirement income. Understanding how your pension is calculated, its distribution options, and its estimated monthly or lump sum payout provisions allows you to plan more wisely.

The average retirement age in America is dropping. Today it's 61½.

The average 61-year-old male is now expected to live to about age 80.

A 61-year-old woman is expected to live even longer. As people continue to retire earlier and live longer, many fear they will outlive their available funds. Financing the years ahead requires planning and astute use of the money you have. Today the average employer-sponsored pension is worth about $5,300 per year, typically in the form of an annuity.

Summary Plan Descriptions

Federal law (ERISA) requires that your pension plan administrators give you, in writing, a Summary Plan Description (SPD). The SPD should be written in clear, understandable terms. It contains information on pension eligibility requirements, accumulation or loss of benefits, filing for benefits, and similar topics. Read your SPD carefully. It provides the information you need to determine how your benefit is computed, election options, and what the plan provides. Take an active role in understanding your pension. Knowing what you'll receive helps to ensure a more confident approach to personal planning.

Types of Pension Plans

There are two basic types of pension plans, a defined benefit (DB) plan and a defined contribution (DC) plan. In a DB plan, the amount of your pension benefit received at retirement is determined in advance by the formula stated in the plan, but the amount contributed to the fund may vary.

In a defined contribution plan, the contributions to the fund are stated, but your actual benefit amount is not known until you retire. Each year you receive an account statement telling you the amount in your account. At retirement you receive a statement of the total amount. Employers contribute and invest money for their employees (plan participants). The funds accumulated for an employee, plus any interest, less annual administrative expenses, make up that participant's pension. Under some plans, such as 401ks, employees also contribute. As the length of your work varies, so does the total amount contributed to the fund. That is why the pension amount received at retirement is not known.

Today many DB pension plans are linked to Social Security benefits. At retirement you receive a pension benefit that is, to some extent, offset by your Social Security benefit. These plans are referred to as integrated plans. They integrate your monthly Social Security benefits and your pension. For instance, some integrated plans compute your monthly pension according to set formulas, and then a percentage of your monthly Social Security benefit is subtracted from the pension amount. The amount remaining is your actual monthly benefit.

From Paternalism to It's Up to You!

More and more companies are moving from DB to DC plans. Pensions, based strictly on years of service and salary, are now rare. Defined contribution plans reflect market conditions and employee initiative. As more options are offered to employees in an attempt to reduce or share costs, a bewildering array of choices and decisions confront employees. They may not be prepared to take responsibility for planning their current and future (retirement) benefits. Many employees are undereducated about their benefits, employer tax-deferred plans, the impact of periodic savings, and the power of compounding.

Pension Trends

No employer provided pension	52%
Defined contribution only	29%
Defined benefit only	12%
Defined benefit and defined contribution	7%

Source: Bureau of Labor Statistics

Vesting

Pension plans usually require employees to meet age and length of service requirements before participating in the plan. Under most plans, you gain a year of service if you work 1,000 hours in 12 consecutive months. This age-plus-service formula varies, but most often it is based on age 21 and one year of service with employers sponsoring the plan.

The length of service requirement or vesting formula (vesting = age +

length of service) determines at what point you are entitled to a certain percentage of the accrued funds in your pension plan. When you are fully vested (100 percent), you are entitled to all the money in your pension. The requirement for being fully vested varies from immediately to three, five, or seven years.

Pension Payments

When you decide to retire, you must choose the type of pension payment that best meets your needs. There are essentially three choices.

- The first, and most popular, is the joint and survivor option. With this choice, you receive a reduced monthly pension check, and your spouse continues to receive a pension check at your death if he or she outlives you.

- The second option is the monthly annuity. If you select this option, you will receive an amount monthly for the remainder of your life but your spouse does not receive any money from your pension plan. If you choose this option, both you and your spouse must endorse the decision, and in most cases the endorsement must be notarized.

- The third choice in some plans is the lump sum. You receive all the money in one payment, including the interest it has earned through the years. If you elect a lump sum payment, do your homework on how to manage it.

Underfunded Pension Plans

The government watchdog on pension underfunding is the Pension Benefit Guaranty Corporation (PBGC) which insures the defined benefit pension plans of corporations. If you have questions about the funding of your pension plan, call the PBGC at 202-326-4000. You can also write to:

U.S. Department of Labor
Division of Technical Assistance and Inquiries
200 Constitution Ave., NW
Washington, DC 20216

Request the publication What You Should Know About Pension Law. The 1997 Retirement Protection Act closes the funding gap created by pension underfunding and requires employers to notify their employees if a pension plan is underfunded.

Tax-Deferred Savings Plans

These are DC plans that allow you to contribute a predetermined portion of your earnings into an account, frequently along with matching contributions from your employer. These plans have become part of most pension plans during the last decade. They combine attributes of an IRA and an employer-sponsored pension plan. Their popularity has been fueled by exceptionally strong stock market performance. Projections show that assets held in DC plans will overtake assets held in DB plans.

There are two principal types of plans: a savings and thrift plan in which an employee contribution is matched in whole or in part by the employer, and a deferred profit-sharing plan in which the employer contributes a portion of profits. In most plans, you can choose your own investments.

These plans often permit employees to defer income and taxes. Your taxable income is reduced by the amount of your contributions. If you're making $40,000 a year and the 401k allows you to contribute up to 25 percent of your salary ($10,000), your W-2 at the end of the year will report taxable income of $30,000. You may be in a lower tax bracket than if you chose not to contribute to the plan. Chances are that you will be in a lower tax bracket at retirement and your 401k distributions will be taxed at this lower rate.

In 2012, the maximum annual deferral under 401k or 403b plans is $17,000 (plus any additional over-50 catch-up provisions). The limit is adjusted annually for inflation in $500 increments.

Payroll Deduction

Your contributions to your savings plan are usually deducted from your paycheck. Using payroll deductions provides the discipline to save. If you don't see it, you don't miss it! Most people at mid-career today probably won't have enough money to retire unless they save more now or work beyond the normal retirement age.

Employer Contributions

Many savings plans have employers matching a percentage of your contributions. This is an incentive by your employer to encourage you to save and increase your self-reliance. You can borrow against the savings plan and pay yourself back, or take a hardship withdrawal if your situation merits one. But beware—any withdrawal (versus a loan) comes with serious penalties, and unpaid loan balances also result in high penalties and taxes.

Portability

These plans are attractive because both your contributions and the earnings belong to you. Often, they can be rolled into another employer's 401k plan or an IRA if you change jobs. If you are vested in the plan, your employer's matching contributions and earnings also belong to you and can also be moved. You may leave the funds with your employer if you meet certain minimum balance requirements. Unless you have a serious and immediate need for cash, you should either roll the funds into another qualified plan or leave them in place.

Your Future and Retirement Benefits

Nothing is guaranteed. Nothing is off limits. Your benefits can change. This is especially true if you are a public sector employee. In mid-2012, San Jose and San Diego, California voted overwhelmingly to cut pension benefits for city workers. Illinois, California, Nevada, and other states are in the process of trying to implement pension reduction measures. In 2013, Federal workers will face very similar pressures as Congress grapples with cutting the deficit

This year a law was enacted that mandated federal employees hired after Dec. 31, 2012, with less than five years of federal service, contribute an additional 2.3 percent of their salary to their FERS pension. This brings their contribution to a total of 3.1 percent. There are now bills in Congress to "pass on" those increases to current employees.

If you are in the private sector, your pension may also be under review as corporate boards deal with the "unfunded" liability issues brought about by aging workforces and a growing retiree population demanding their benefits. So begin now to build a self reliant financial base. Keep your life expenses down and your savings contributions up. When you are in your 30s and 40s, begin projecting what you may need when you do retire. Do a gap analysis to assess your "shortfall", and begin that long term savings and investment process now.

CHAPTER 8

Your Federal Benefits

What's going to change and how can I plan for it?
What are the options for withdrawing TSP funds?
How will my FERS benefits impact my Social Security?
Is a full survivor benefit the smartest way to go?
When is the Roth Thrift option available?

I t is important to have a clear understanding of what you are entitled to long before retirement. Often employees discover that their planning began too late and they find themselves pressured to understand choices and make decisions in a very short timeframe. If you have not begun to plan, you need to make it a high priority. If your planning is underway, you need to evaluate those plans and make any necessary course corrections.

The following questions come up most often as employees begin looking at how their federal pension and benefits will impact their future:

- What counts toward total service time (eligibility requirements)?
- What are my options for taking my traditional TSP or Roth money at retirement?
- How will my annuity be computed and how are survivor benefits factored in?
- Can I estimate how much I'll receive at retirement?
- What do I need to know about carrying my life and health insurance into retirement?

If you were hired after Jan. 1, 1984, you are under the Federal Employees Retirement System (FERS). FERS was designed to acknowledge that today's federal workforce is more transient. Social Security is one of three components of FERS. If you change careers, your Social Security travels with you. This portability is important in a workforce where the average 40-year-old has already had eight different jobs.

The second component of FERS is the Basic Benefit Plan or pension. It is the smallest of the three components of your retirement plan.

The third component, the Thrift Savings Plan, shifts much of the responsibility for a financially secure future from the government's shoulders to yours. Since 1987, federal employees have had the opportunity to participate in the Thrift Savings Plan. If you are under FERS your maximum contribution is now guided by a dollar amount that changes yearly. In 2012 the maximum "IRS regulated" contribution is $17,000. The government matches the first 5 percent the employee contributes. The money you have withheld is all tax deferred. If you opt for the tax free Roth Thrift option, your money is not tax deductable, but earnings and principal can the withdrawn tax free. Over time this can add up to a very sizable nest egg. From the government's standpoint, the Thrift Plan means your financial future is now more of a planning partnership. If you don't do your part in funding your TSP account, your future may be less secure.

The Federal Employees Retirement System was first available to employees in the Open Season of 1987 when some CSRS employees transferred into FERS. All federal employees first hired after January 1984 are automatically FERS employees. FERS covers:

- Anyone first hired or rehired (with a break in service of one year or more and less than five years of civilian service) after Dec. 31, 1983;
- Employees rehired from Jan. 1, 1984, through Dec. 31, 1986, who had less than five years of civilian service on Dec. 31, 1986; and
- Employees who elected to transfer from CSRS.

If you retire under FERS, you have three sources of retirement funds: Social Security, a FERS annuity, and your Thrift Savings Plan account.

Social Security. Like employees in the private sector, you contribute 7.65 percent of your salary to the Social Security system. Of your contribution, 6.2 percent is a Social Security tax, although in 2011, that contribution drops to 4.2% for that year only. Medicare is 1.45 percent. When you become eligible for Social Security, contributions from the current workforce will provide your benefit. If you leave federal service before retirement your Social Security travels with you to your new employer.

The Basic Benefit Plan. FERS regular employees contribute 0.8 percent of their salary to the Basic Benefit Plan or FERS Basic Annuity, administered by OPM. This contribution rate may increase for current employees, and does increase for anyone hired after January 1, 2013.

The Thrift Savings Plan. The final source of FERS retirement funds is the Thrift Savings Plan, which is administered by the Thrift Investment Board. The contribution limit is a dollar amount established annually by the Internal Revenue Service (IRS).

When am I eligible to retire?

If you have five or more years of creditable service under FERS or a combination of both CSRS and FERS, you are vested and have a right to receive benefits from the retirement system. Your benefit is an annuity when age and service requirements are met. To receive disability or to provide a survivor benefit you need 18 months of service.

FERS Minimum Retirement Age (MRA)

Year of Birth	MRA	Year of Birth	MRA
Before 1948	55	1965	56 & 2 mo.
1948	55 & 2 mo.	1966	56 & 4 mo.
1949	55 & 4 mo.	1967	56 & 6 mo.
1950	55 & 6 mo.	1968	56 & 8 mo.
1951	55 & 8 mo.	1969	56 & 10 mo.
1952	55 & 10 mo.	1970+	57
1953-64	56		

Retirement	Age	Years of Service
Optional/Voluntary	MRA	30
	60	20
	62	5
	MRA	+10*

* Your annuity will be reduced 5% for each year you are under age 62. Deferred Annuity payable at age 62 with five years of service

Retirement	Age	Years of Service
Involuntary/ Early Optional	50	20
(Discontinued Service)	Any Age	25
Deferred	62	5
	60	20
	MRA	30
	MRA	+10
Disability	Any Age	10 months

Many employees choose not to take a deferred annuity and, instead, withdraw all the money they've contributed when they leave federal service. With even moderate inflation, taking a deferred annuity means that those dollars won't buy as much at age 62 as they might today. Think carefully about whether to leave the money in or take it out. If you choose to withdraw all of your contributions at the time of separation, the money will be paid to you with a market rate of interest. However, if you are subsequently reemployed under FERS, you will not be able to use the previous FERS employment for retirement purposes. **Refunds under FERS permanently extinguish service credit.** As a general rule, it's usually wisest to leave the money in the system, taking it as a deferred annuity. This is because you pay very little compared to the benefits you will receive — only about 5 percent of the total value of your Basic Benefits.

What if I quit before retirement?

Employees who leave federal service before retirement have three options. They can take a deferred annuity at 62 as long as they have 5 or more years of service. They could take a refund of their total FERS contributions with market rate interest applied to that refund. The last option is they could let their contributions stay in the FERS system if they feel they may work for the federal government again at some future date. They would still retain the right to remove contributions at any point

What service counts toward retirement?

The largest part of FERS creditable service, for most people, is all time between the date they were hired and the date of separation. Any employee who began a federal career after January 1984 is automatically covered by FERS. Any CSRS employee who transferred to FERS between July and December 1987 has been covered by FERS since the date of their transfer. If you transferred with at least five years of vested CSRS service, part of your annuity will be computed under CSRS and part will be computed under FERS. If you transferred with less than five years of service, all of your time is considered to be FERS service. A federal employee subject to the CSRS interim provisions during 1984-86 paid 1.3 percent CSRS salary deductions and full Social Security deductions. This service can also be counted as FERS creditable service for an employee who transferred to FERS.

As a general rule, any **active military service** that ended with an honorable discharge can be credited toward your FERS retirement. Any military service occurring after 1956, mandates you must pay 3 percent of your total base military pay, plus interest, for that service to be credited toward your retirement. Your military time is then added to your total FERS service and significantly increases your annuity payout.

Interest charges will not be added to what you owe for military service if you make the deposit within the three-year interest-free period. Interest starts and is compounded annually beginning two years from the date first employed. The earliest possible interest posting for an unpaid military service deposit is Jan. 1, 1990. The interest rate has been variable (money market rates) since 1985. No credit is allowed for any period of retired military service unless the retiree waives receipt of military retired pay. The retiree does not have to waive retired pay awarded based on a service-connected disability incurred in combat, or based on age and service in the reserves.

FERS Sick Leave Rules. Employees covered by FERS can now apply their unused sick leave to their years of service for retirement purposes. FERS employees' unused sick leave can be credited towards their length of service. Unused sick leave cannot be used to reach eligibility to retire; however, it will be used to calculate the amount of the annuity received. Sick leave can only be credited in 30 day increments. Currently, FERS employees get a 50% credit for their sick leave. Beginning in 2014, FERS employees will get 100% credit.

CSRS/FERS Sick Leave Sick Leave Chart

Chart for Obtaining Number of Days/Months When 2,087 Hours Constitutes Yearly Basis

Days	1 Day and up	1 mo. and up	2 mo. and up	3 mo. and up	4 mo. and up	5 mo. and up	6 mo. and up	7 mo. and up	8 mo. and up	9 mo. and up	10 mo. and up	11 mo. and up
0	0	174	348	522	696	870	1044	1217	1391	1565	1739	1913
1	6	180	354	528	701	875	1049	1223	1397	1571	1745	1919
2	12	186	359	533	707	881	1055	1229	1403	1577	1751	1925
3	17	191	365	539	713	887	1061	1235	1409	1583	1757	1930
4	23	197	371	545	719	893	1067	1241	1415	1588	1762	1936
5	29	203	377	551	725	899	1072	1246	1420	1594	1768	1942
6	35	209	383	557	730	904	1078	1252	1426	1600	1774	1948
7	41	214	388	562	736	910	1084	1258	1432	1606	1780	1954
8	46	220	394	568	742	916	1090	1264	1438	1612	1786	1959
9	52	226	400	574	748	922	1096	1270	1444	1617	1791	1965
10	58	232	406	580	754	928	1101	1275	1449	1623	1797	1971
11	64	238	412	586	759	933	1107	1281	1455	1629	1803	1977
12	70	243	417	591	765	939	1113	1287	1461	1635	1809	1983
13	75	249	423	597	771	945	1119	1293	1467	1641	1815	1988
14	81	255	429	603	777	951	1125	1299	1472	1646	1820	1994
15	87	261	435	609	783	957	1130	1304	1478	1652	1826	2000
16	93	267	441	615	788	962	1136	1310	1484	1658	1832	2006
17	99	272	446	620	794	968	1142	1316	1490	1664	1838	2012
18	104	278	452	626	800	974	1148	1322	1496	1670	1844	2017
19	110	284	458	632	806	980	1154	1328	1501	1675	1849	2023
20	116	293	464	638	812	986	1159	1333	1507	1681	1855	2029
21	122	296	470	643	817	991	1165	1339	1513	1687	1861	2035
22	128	301	475	649	823	997	1171	1345	1519	1693	1867	2041
23	133	307	481	655	829	1003	1177	1351	1525	1699	1873	2046
24	139	313	487	661	835	1009	1183	1357	1530	1704	1878	2052
25	145	319	493	667	841	1015	1188	1362	1536	1710	1884	2058
26	151	325	499	672	846	1020	1194	1368	1542	1716	1890	2064
27	157	330	504	678	852	1026	1200	1374	1548	1722	1896	2070
28	162	336	510	684	858	1032	1206	1380	1554	1728	1901	2075
29	168	342	516	690	864	1038	1212	1386	1559	1733	1907	2081

- **Other Creditable Service.** Credit is generally given for both civilian and military service performed for the federal government.
- **Leave Without Pay** (LWOP). Other creditable service can include periods of leave without pay. Credit is given for up to six months per calendar year.
- **Part-Time Employment.** For eligibility, full credit is granted for all time between the date of hire and the date of separation for part-time service. The annuity is computed by determining the percentage of time you worked over your entire federal career times the high-3 that you would have earned if you had been full-time.
- **Deposit Service**. Any period of civilian service not covered by FERS is called deposit or non-deduction service. To be creditable for both retirement eligibility and annuity computation, the non-deduction service must have been performed prior to Jan. 1, 1989, and a deposit must be made. If you leave federal service and receive a refund on your retirement contributions, and later return to government work, that service is called redeposit service. FERS employees are now permitted to redeposit funds into the retirement system to replace money they had previously withdrawn. A redeposit will have associated interest costs.

If you withdraw your FERS retirement contributions after you separate, you forfeit the ability to receive credit for that period of service should you later return to federal employment unless you repay your retirement contributions and accrued interest.

How much will my annuity be?

The FERS Basic Benefit Plan provides retirement benefits based on years of service, age, and your average high-3. An employee with enough years of service can retire at the minimum retirement age and receive unreduced benefits.

An employee can retire at age 62 with five or more years of service, at age 60 with 20 or more years of service, or at the MRA (minimum retirement age) with 30 or more years of service. Computing your FERS annuity is relatively easy. The amount you receive when you leave federal service, or retire, is a combination of your Social Security, your Basic Annuity, and your contributions to the Thrift Plan.

Depending on your age and your years of service at retirement, different computation formulas apply. If you retire before age 62, the following computation formula is used:

1% x average high-3 x Years & Months of Service

If you retire at age 62 or later, with less than 20 years of service, the computation formula is:

1% x average high-3 x Years & Months of Service

If you retire at age 62 or later, with 20 or more years of service, use the following formula:

1.1% x average high-3 x Years & Months of Service

For a 57-year-old employee with 30 years of service and a high-3 average salary of $60,000, the calculation is:

1% x $60,000 x 30 years
$600 x 30 = $18,000

If you elect to receive the monthly benefit at the Minimum Retirement Age, and if you have at least 10 but less than 30 years of service, the benefit will be permanently reduced 5 percent a year for each year you are under 62.

If you leave federal service before retirement, you can withdraw your retirement contributions. If you do, you forfeit the ability to receive credit for that period of service under FERS should you later return to federal employment.

What is a deferred annuity?

If you leave federal employment after five years of creditable service for any reason other than death, disability, or retirement, and you do not withdraw your contributions from FERS, you will be eligible to receive **deferred benefits** from the FERS Basic Benefit Plan once you reach age 62. If you are eligible for the deferred benefit, you can begin to receive the benefit (with reductions, prior to age 62) at any time after you meet your MRA with 10 years of service. If you elect to receive a deferred benefit prior to age 62, your annuity will be permanently reduced 5 percent for each year you are under age 62.

Can I retire early?

You can retire with fewer years of service and receive reduced retirement benefits if you have reached your MRA and completed at least 10 years of service, including five years of civilian service. If, as a FERS employee, you do retire early, your annuity is permanently reduced 5 percent for every year you are below age 62. You can defer receipt of your annuity until age 62, however, and reduce or eliminate the 5 percent per year reduction.

What happens if I am disabled?

To qualify for disability under FERS, you must be totally disabled for useful and efficient service in the position you currently occupy and for service in any vacant position in the agency at the same grade and pay level and in the same commuting area. The determination of total disability is made by OPM when information in the file indicates that there is a service deficiency caused by disease or injury of sufficient degree to preclude useful and efficient service. The disability must be expected to last at least one year or terminate in death. There is no age requirement to apply for a FERS disability retirement, but you must have at least 18 months of creditable civilian service and you must file for Social Security disability.

Disability Computation. An employee under age 62 is entitled to:

- First year: 60 percent of high-3 average salary minus 100 percent of any Social Security benefits payable
- Second and subsequent years until age 62: 40 percent of high-3 minus 60 percent of any Social Security benefits payable

The month the retiree reaches age 62, the disability annuity is recomputed using the basic annuity formula (1 percent if less than 20 years of service or 1.1 percent if 20 or more years times the high-3). The retiree receives additional service credit for the total time on the disability retirement rolls. The high-3 average salary is increased by all FERS COLAs the retiree received during retirement.

When an employee age 62 or older applies for disability retirement, they receive their earned annuity based on total years of creditable service and high-3 average salary. **No COLAs are provided during the first year on the disability rolls if receiving 60 percent of the high-3.**

What will my survivors receive?

Employee Death. The spouse of an employee with at least 18 months of creditable civilian but less than 10 years of total service that dies after

Dec. 1, 2011, and before Dec.1, 2012, receives a payment of $30,792.98, indexed each year for inflation. This payment can be taken as a lump sum or in 36 monthly installments. The spouse also receives the larger of either:

- 50 percent of the final annual salary at the time of death, or
- 50 percent of the high-3.

The surviving spouse is also potentially eligible for the deceased employee's Social Security benefits and TSP death benefits. The spouse of a deceased employee with 10 years or more of service will receive the above benefits, plus an annuity equal to 50 percent of the employee's accrued basic benefit. The employee's children receive an amount that varies depending upon the number of children. Benefits are reduced by any Social Security benefits that are received. The following rates for children's benefits apply from Dec. 1, 2011, through Nov. 30, 2012. When the child has a living parent who was married to the employee or retiree, the benefit payable is the lesser of $486 per month per child; or $1,460 per month divided by the number of eligible children (if more than three).

Annuitant Death. At the time of retirement, an employee must elect one of the following three options to establish postretirement survivor benefits:

- **Full survivor benefit.** Base annuity reduced by 10 percent. Your survivor receives 50 percent of your base annuity for life unless they remarry prior to age 55. However, if the marriage lasted for at least 30 years, the survivor annuity will not be terminated.
- **One-half survivor benefit.** Base annuity reduced by 5 percent. Survivor receives 25 percent of your base annuity for life unless they remarry prior to age 55. However, if the marriage lasted for at least 30 years, the survivor annuity will not be terminated.
- **No survivor benefit.** Base annuity not reduced. Survivor receives no benefit.

Elections other than a full benefit require spousal consent. **If at least a partial survivor benefit is not elected, your spouse will be ineligible to continue FEHB coverage after your death.** Postretirement death and preretirement death benefits for eligible children are the same.

What is the Special Annuity Supplement?

The Special Annuity Supplement is a bridge payment to be paid from the time you retire until age 62.

At age 62 the payment stops, and Social Security begins. The supplement is subject to the same earnings test as is used with Social Security benefits. It is paid to employees who retire with an immediate benefit at the MRA after at least 30 years of service; at age 60 after at least 20 years of service; and on retirement under the special provisions relating to law enforcement, firefighters, and air-traffic controllers.

The supplement is calculated by first estimating your full career (40 years) Social Security benefit. It then approximates the amount of that benefit that was earned while working under FERS. The formula is:

(Estimated Social Security Benefit) x (Years of FERS Civilian Service) ÷ by 40

If you decide to retire at age 60 and your full career Social Security benefit at age 62 is equal to $12,000 a year, and you worked in service covered under FERS for 20 years, the proportion earned under FERS is equal to 20 years divided by 40 (full career) or .50. The supplement would be calculated as follows:

Estimated Social Security Benefit x Years of Service ÷ 40 = FERS Supplement
$12,000 x 20 ÷ 40 = $6,000
$12,000 x .50 = $6,000

Therefore, you would receive, in addition to the FERS basic annuity, a Special Retirement Supplement of $6,000 per year. The supplement is available only if you retire before age 62 and is only paid until you reach age 62.

The Earnings Test

If you retire under FERS before age 62, but you are employed elsewhere after retirement, you may lose all or part of the supplement. The reduction depends on your level of earnings after retirement. The reduction applies to the supplement only, not the basic benefit. A retiree can have a minimum level of earnings without losing any of the supplement. If the earnings are above the minimum level, however, the supplement will be reduced. OPM will ask you for a statement of earnings each year you are eligible to receive the supplement.

COLAs

Both CSRS and FERS retirees receive cost-of-living adjustments (COLAs).

The amount of the COLA is determined by comparing the Consumer Price Index for Wage Earners and Clerical Workers (CPI-W) for the third calendar quarter of the current year with the same calendar quarter of the preceding year. Under CSRS the resulting percentage will be applied to the retiree or survivor annuity effective December 1 and payable in the January check.

CSRS retirees and survivors will receive a full COLA. FERS retirees do not receive a COLA until they are age 62 unless they retire on FERS disability. Disability retirees receive a COLA after one year on the disability rolls. The FERS COLA is generally referred to as a COLA minus one. Actually, if the percentage is greater than 3 percent, it is a COLA minus one; if it is between 2 percent and 3 percent, the COLA will be 2 percent; if it is less than 2 percent, the full COLA will be paid.

Annual COLAs are prorated, depending upon the number of months the recipient has been retired.

The Lump Sum

At retirement all retirees receive a lump sum payment for all remaining annual leave accrued during the current leave year. You will also receive a lump sum payment for annual leave carried over from previous years. The lump sum payment is calculated by multiplying the number of hours of leave by your hourly rate of pay, plus other types of pay you would have received while on annual leave, excluding any allowances that are paid for the sole purpose of retaining a federal employee in government service. Locality pay or other similar geographic adjustments and across-the-board annual adjustments are included in the lump sum payment.

Health Benefits (FEHB)

Your eligibility to continue group health benefits is an important factor to consider when planning retirement. The Federal Employees Health Benefits program is a voluntary contributory program, open to almost all employees. The federal government contributes to the cost of the plans with employees paying their share through payroll deductions.

Employees are offered various group plans, which reduce the cost of health care services, including coverage for prolonged illness or serious accidents.

You can enroll in the plan of your choice. If you elect to enroll but later wish to change enrollment, you may do so only during the annual open season. If you elect not to enroll when eligible for coverage, you must wait for an event — e.g., changes in marital/family status or relocating from an area served by an HMO — to enroll or make an enrollment change.

Dental and Vision

Dental and vision insurance is like other insurance options, you make the selections during the open enrollment season. You can pay for these benefits using pre-tax dollars. The dental and vision benefits are not subsidized by the government. The size of the federal workforce meant OPM could negotiate better rates of coverage.

All plans offer three enrollment options: yourself, yourself plus one, or yourself plus family. As with insurance, compare the government rate with those from the open market. You may find less expensive coverage in the open market. Federal employees have waited a long time for these benefits and all indications suggest they will be well received.

Continuing FEHB

Your FEHB can continue into retirement provided the following requirements are met:

1. You retire on an immediate annuity, and
2. You have been enrolled or covered as a family member in a plan covered by the health benefits program for five years of service immediately preceding your retirement, or for all service since your first enrollment opportunity. The time you are covered under the **Uniformed Service Health Benefits Program** (TRICARE) is considered a federal plan for continuous coverage as long as you are covered under an FEHB enrollment at the time of your retirement.

There is an automatic waiver of the minimum enrollment of five years for certain employees retiring with buyouts or taking early optional retirement. For inquiries, call this special OPM number: 202-606-0191. As a retiree, you're entitled to the same benefits and government contributions as any active employee in the same health plan. Your costs will be the same as those of active employees and are usually deducted from your annuity. Your agency will automatically transfer the enrollment to OPM. You don't need to do anything unless you want to make changes in the coverage.

Now you can also cover adult children (unmarried or married) under your FEHB coverage until they are 26 years of age.

Temporary Continuation of Coverage

If you leave federal service before you retire, or are ineligible to carry the coverage into retirement, you are eligible to enroll in the Temporary Continuation of Coverage program (TCC). This program allows a separated employee to continue coverage under FEHB without a break for up to 18 months from the date of his/her separation. You will be responsible for paying both your share and the government share of the premium plus an administrative fee of approximately 2 percent of the premium. You are allowed 60 days from the date of separation in which to make this decision.

Life Insurance (FEGLI)

The Federal Employees Group Life Insurance (FEGLI) program offers two kinds of term life insurance, providing benefits upon the death of the insured — Basic Life Insurance or Optional Life Insurance.

Basic Life Insurance

The Basic option provides an amount of coverage based on your annual basic salary, which includes locality pay. All eligible employees are automatically covered for basic life insurance under the FEGLI program, unless it is specifically waived.

- Equal to annual basic pay (rounded to next $1,000, plus $2,000)
- Double life insurance benefits until age 36, decreasing at 10 percent per year until age 45 at which time extra coverage will end
- Accidental death and dismemberment coverage while an active employee, no accidental death and dismemberment coverage in retirement

Optional Life Insurance

Additional optional insurance may be elected within 60 days of being permanently hired. Basic Life must have been elected to be eligible for Optional Life.

- **Option A:** Standard: Additional $10,000 life insurance coverage, additional $10,000 accidental death and dismemberment coverage until retirement

- **Option B:** Additional: Additional life insurance coverage equal to one, two, three, four, or five times actual rate of basic pay (rounded to next $1,000
- **Option C:** Family: Additional life insurance coverage equal to one, two, three, four, or five times $5,000 on your spouse and $2,500 on eligible children

If you do not want Basic Life and/or Optional Life insurance, you can decline it by submitting the proper form to the Personnel Office. If, at a later date, you decide on insurance coverage, you can request it if you meet the following requirements:

- At least one year must have elapsed between the effective date of your last waiver (or declination) and the date of the request for insurance.
- You must furnish, at your expense, adequate medical evidence of insurability.

If you leave federal employment before you retire or have completed twelve months in a non-pay status, you have 60 days to convert to an individual, non-group policy. Life insurance coverage can be continued into retirement provided certain requirements are met.

Insurance	$ at retirement	At age 65 & retired
Basic 75% Reduction	$.3250/$1,000 of BIA*	No cost. Starts to reduce 2% per month; reduces down to 25% of amount at retirement.
Basic 50% Reduction	$.9650 per $1,000	Cost is $.64 per $1,000 of BIA. Starts to reduce 1% per month; reduces to 50% of amount at retirement.
Basic No Reduction	$2.2650 per $1,000	Cost is $1.94 per $1,000 of BIA. No reduction in coverage.
Standard Option A	Premiums based on age band**	No cost. Coverage reduces 2% per month until it reaches 25% of preretirement amount. ($2,500).
Additional Option B	Premiums based on age band**	Full Reduction. No Cost. Coverage Option B starts to reduce 2% per month until coverage ends. No Reduction. Premiums continue

		to be withheld from annuity based on age band.
Family Option C	Premiums based on age band** and number of multiples	Full Reduction-No cost. Coverage reduces 2% per month until coverage ends.
		No Reduction. Premiums continue to be withheld based on age band.

* *Basic Insurance Amount is your final annual basic pay, rounded to the next exact $1,000, plus $2,000. Your BIA reduces after you are retired and are age 65, unless you have elected No Reduction.*

** *Consult OPM or your agency for the age bands.*

Age Bands: Monthly Withholding Costs

Age Group	Option A-Standard	Option B-Additional	Option C-Family
Under age 35	$ 0.65	$0.043	$ 0.48
35-39	$ 0.87	$0.065	$ 0.63
40-44	$ 1.30	$0.108	$ 0.91
45-49	$ 1.95	$0.173	$ 1.37
50-54	$ 3.03	$0.282	$ 2.04
55-59	$ 5.85	$0.498	$ 3.29
60-64	$13.00	$1.27	$ 5.85
65-69	—	$1.34	$ 6.80
70-74	—	$2.47	$ 7.80
75-79	—	$3.90	$ 10.40
80+	—	$5.20	$14.30

Designating Beneficiaries. You do not need to name a beneficiary if you wish to have death benefits paid in the following order of precedence:

1. Your widow or widower
2. Your child or children in equal shares, with the share of any deceased child distributed among the descendants of that child
3. Your parents in equal shares or the entire amount to the surviving parent
4. The duly appointed executor or administrator of your estate

5. Your next of kin under the laws of your domicile at the time of your death

If you do wish to name a beneficiary, and you are survived by a designated beneficiary, the benefits will be paid to the beneficiary. To name a beneficiary or change a prior designation, complete a new designation. The designation must be as follows:

1. Signed by you
2. Witnessed by two persons, neither of whom is a beneficiary (a witness to the designation may not receive payment as a beneficiary)
3. Received by your employing office (for employees) or retirement system (for annuitants) before your death

Death benefits, in the event of an employee death, are paid from four sources:
1. Federal Employees Group Life Insurance (FEGLI)
2. Civil Service Retirement System or Federal Employees Retirement System
3. Unpaid Compensation (unused annual leave and unpaid salary)
4. Thrift Savings Plan

If you do wish to name a beneficiary other than those listed, or if you do not wish to follow the order of precedence, complete a designation of beneficiary form for the type of fund for which you wish to designate. You may request the following designations of beneficiary forms from your servicing Personnel Office: SF 2823 for FEGLI, SF 2808 for CSRS, SF 3102 for FERS, SF 1152 for Unpaid Compensation of a Deceased Civilian Employee, and Form TSP-3 for the Thrift Savings Plan. It is important that designations be kept current in order that death benefits are paid in accordance with your wishes.

Long-Term-Care Insurance

This insurance has been available for almost 10 years. There are currently no open seasons scheduled, but you may still make an application. If you have aging parents or are concerned about your own long-term-care needs the government program is worth exploring. Information and application forms are available at www.ltcfeds.com or by calling 1-800-582-3337.

Who is eligible?

Federal employees, retirees, survivor annuitants, adult children, spouses, and parents of employees are eligible participants. Newly hired employees and members of the uniformed services and their spouses are subject to the short form of underwriting consisting of several general health questions. Current employees and retirees are subject to the long form of underwriting.

The program is offered by **Long Term Care Partners**, a partnership of **John Hancock Life Insurance Company** and **Metropolitan Life Insurance Company**. The premium amount is determined by the enrollee's age at the time LTC Partners receives your application and the plan you choose. OPM has posted a list of Frequently Asked Questions (FAQ) about the new insurance at **www.opm.gov**. The insurance has four basic options.

Available Plans		*Monthly Premiums*	
		45-year-old	*60-year-old*
Facilities 100	3 years coverage at $100/day	$11.00	$27.80
Comprehensive 100	3 years coverage at $150/day	$16.40	$40.60
Comprehensive 150	5 years coverage at $150/day	$28.50	$72.30
Comprehensive 150+	5 years coverage at $150/day with unlimited coverage	$37.20	$94.20

Note: Plans include 4% automatic compound inflation option.

The waiting period before benefits can begin is 90 days on all three plans. Benefit amounts can be customized in $50 increments (from $100 a day to a maximum of $450). Enrollees can select 4 or 5 percent, automatic inflation protection, or elect to have benefits remain the same but have the opportunity to purchase additional coverage, at higher prices, every two years. Premiums will be based on age, and the cost for employees recently retired and those eligible for retirement will be higher.

Premiums will also be affected by which benefits are chosen, the length of the policy, the waiting period, and the inflation protection selected. Employees and retirees will pay the entire premium. There will be no employer contribution. The coverage is guaranteed renewable and is also portable at the same premium.

What are the benefits?

Enrollees select a maximum benefit and policy length. The maximum daily benefit is $100 to $450. Policy length can be two, three or five years or lifetime. The choices you make in benefits and policy length will determine your "pool of money." The LTC insurance will pay benefits until your "pool of money" is exhausted. The lifetime choice has an inexhaustible "pool of money."

You will be eligible to receive benefits when you meet one of the following two conditions and you satisfy the waiting period you selected.

- You cannot perform two of six activities of daily living and your doctor certifies that the condition is expected to last at least 90 days, or
- You have severe cognitive impairment.

Flexible Spending Accounts

Recently the federal government introduced Flexible Spending Accounts (FSA) for health care. Here's how they work. At the beginning of each year, you elect to defer monies into a savings account. The maximum limit in 2012 is $5,000. When you incur an eligible expense, you simply complete a claim form and submit it (with receipts) for reimbursement from your FSA. You are using pretax dollars to pay for items that are typically not covered by your insurance:

- Medical and dental visits not covered by insurance
- Co-payments
- Deductibles
- Eyeglasses

The most compelling reason to set up an FSA is that by using pretax dollars, you spend less and have more of what you earn to spend on what you want or need.

The down side of FSAs is that it's a "use it or lose it" proposition. If you have any money left in the account after all claims have been paid for the year, you forfeit it. This means you need to use caution in determining how much you will contribute each year. If you find that by mid-November there is a lot of money still in your FSA, you are apt to make purchases that you would not normally make. A second set of prescription sunglasses or an extra chiropractic adjustment is not the best use of your funds. The plan works if you plan carefully and spend down all of the funds each year.

In addition to a medical saving account, you can set up a dependent care FSA for expenses you incur for the care of children under age 13 and dependent adults. The maximum allotment for 2011 is $6,000 if you are married and filing a joint tax return, or $3,000 if you file an individual tax return.

Thrift Savings Plan

All federal employees are eligible to participate in the Thrift Savings Plan (TSP). You can participate in either the traditional Thrift tax deferred plan, or the new Roth option, or both.

The traditional Thrift Plan is like a 401k plan and has two major tax advantages. First, your contributions reduce your gross income for federal and, in most cases, state income tax purposes. Second, you do not pay current federal income taxes on the earnings on the TSP account until you withdraw the funds. You can continue to defer taxes after leaving federal employment if you transfer the money into an IRA or other qualified plan. If you have at least five years of service, and $3,500 in your account, you can defer withdrawals and leave the account open with the Thrift Investment Board. You can also leave money in the TSP if you're subject to a RIF even if you have less than five years of service. These funds are tax deferred not tax free. When you begin taking distributions you may be in a lower tax bracket. Even if your TSP account is taxed as income, which can usually be minimized, compounding for 20 or more years is well worth the possible tax impact later.

Your Thrift Savings Plan account is valued on a daily, rather than a monthly basis. This allows you to transfer money among the available funds as often as once a day. In addition, account balances are being converted to shares initially valued at $10 each for all funds.

TSP contributions are based on IRS limits instead of percentage of employee wage. The 2012 IRS limit is $17,000 ($22,500 for those over age 50). Increases for 2012 and beyond will be indexed. **Note: Make sure your FERS contributions are spread over the full calendar year. Agency matching contributions are based on the first 5 percent of your contributions withheld each pay period. If you reach the IRS**

limit on Sept. 30 you would lose the agency matching contributions for October through December.

Your contribution is deducted from your pay before federal income tax is computed. Thus, money put into the Thrift Savings Plan is not included on the year end W-2 form. This means that your taxable earnings are lower and you pay less in income tax. This does not affect your gross earnings as a basis for calculating retirement, leave, or Social Security taxes.

The TSP accepts rollovers from 401k plans and conduit IRAs. Participants will deal directly with the TSP Service Office. You still cannot rollover money from a regular IRA, a mutual fund, or savings account. Rollover forms are available on the TSP web site or from the TSP Service Office.

The Thrift Savings Plan allows employees age 50 and over to make additional contributions to the TSP under the **catch-up** provision. The legislation allows those employees who contribute the maximum to their TSP accounts to contribute another $6,000 in 2012 through payroll deductions. Thus, an employee over 50 could contribute $22,500 to the TSP. The catch-up contribution is not matched by the federal government and follows the allocation already in force in your TSP account.

Because the limits for contributions to the Thrift Savings Plan change each year you will have to complete a Form TSP-1-C each year to elect to make the catch-up contributions.

Roth TSP Option

The Roth TSP was finally introduced in 2012. It has more tax flexibility than the traditional TSP. Now Federal workers can contribute to both the Roth and the traditional TSP. Roth contributions are taken out of your paycheck after you income is taxed. When you withdraw funds from your Roth balance, you receive your Roth contributions tax-free since you already paid taxes on the contributions. That can have a very positive impact on your retirement income.

You do have to meet certain criteria to withdraw Roth TSP contributions. You have to be at least age 59½ (or disabled) and your withdrawal must be made at least 5 years after the beginning of the year in which you made your first Roth contribution.

The money already in your TSP account when you begin making Roth

Contributions will remain part of your traditional TSP balance. You cannot convert traditional TSP balances. You cannot convert traditional existing TSP monies to a Roth, because that creates a "taxable event".

The IRS mandated combined total contribution rate to your Roth and traditional TSP is $17,000 in 2012 and $22,500 if you are over 50. Your agency contributions will always be part of the traditional (non-Roth) balances. Any contribution allocation or inter-fund transfer will apply to the investment of both your Roth and traditional TSP contributions or balances.

You will be able to take loans, in-service withdrawals, and partial withdrawals from your account. If you do this they will come out of your account on a pro rata basis with a proportional amount from your traditional and Roth balances.

If you had a Roth with a previous employer like a Roth 401(k), Roth 403(b), or Roth 457(b), these funds could be transferred into your TSP Roth. If you have an individual Roth IRA, those funds cannot be transferred to the TSP Roth.

Finally, when you begin to withdraw TSP funds you will be able to separately transfer any portion of your Roth and your traditional balances to IRA's or other eligible employer plans.

The following chart provides a snapshot of the differences between the traditional TSP and the Roth option.

The Treatment of	Traditional TSP	Roth TSP
Contributions	**Pre-tax**	**After-tax**[1]
Your Paycheck	**Taxes are deferred**, so less money is taken out of your paycheck	**Taxes are paid up front**, so more money comes out of your paycheck
Transfers In	**Transfers**, allowed from eligible employer plans and traditional IRAs	**Transfers**, allowed from Roth 401(k)s, Roth 403(b)s, Roth 457(b)s, and Roth IRAs[3]

Transfers Out	*Transfers* allowed to eligible employer plans and traditional IRAs, and Roth IRAs[2]	*Transfers* allowed to Roth 401(k)s, Roth 403(b)s, Roth 457(b)s, and Roth IRAs[3]
Withdrawals	*Taxable* when withdrawn	*Tax-free* earnings if five years have passed since Januray 1 of the year you made your first Roth contribution, AND you are age 59½ or older, permanently disabled, or deceased

The Thrift Savings Plan currently offers five investment fund options (Lifecycle, or L Funds). The funds differ in risk and potential return:

Fund I: International Stock Index Investment Fund — invested in Barclay's EAFE Index Fund, which tracks the Europe, Australasia, and Far East (EAFE) stock index. In a global economy some markets grow at faster rates. This fund allows investors to tap into fast-growing foreign markets. These markets are subject to currency and interest rate fluctuations. This means greater instability. The I Fund will, therefore, be riskier than the C, F, and G funds, but it will also offer the potential for greater reward.

Fund S: Small Capitalization Stock Investment Fund — the small-cap fund consists of stock of small companies with growth potential. Like the I fund, the S Fund will carry greater risk since small-company stock can be quite volatile. It is invested in Barclay's Extended Market Index Fund, which tracks the Wilshire 4500 stock index.

Fund C: Common Stock Index Investment Fund — invested in Barclay's Equity Index Fund, which tracks the Standard and Poor's 500 Stock Index. The index includes 500 stocks, representing 84 separate industries. All are U.S. stocks, and most are traded on the New York Stock Exchange. This fund provides the opportunity to earn greater returns, but it also involves more risk. Investment earnings will fluctuate, according to market conditions, and the principal amount is not guaranteed.

Fund F: Fixed-Income Investment Fund — invested in Barclay's U.S. Debt Index fund which tracks the Lehman Brothers Aggregate Bond Index. This option aims at matching the performance of the U.S. bond market.

Fund G: Government Securities Investment Fund — invested in U.S. Government securities. It is risk-free with a competitive rate of return.

Federal employees and retirees investing in the Thrift Savings Plan are continuing to invest more heavily in the common stock fund (C Fund) than in the bond fund (F Fund) or the government securities fund (G Fund).

Rates of Return for TSP Investment Funds (Lifecycle Funds)

	2011	2010	2009
Fund G	2.45%	2.81	2.97%
Fund F	7.89%	6.71%	5.99%
Fund C	2.11%	15.06%	26.68%
Fund S	(3.38%)	29.06%	34.85%
Fund I	(11.81%)	7.94%	30.04%
L2020	.041%	10.59%	19.14%
L2030	(.031%)	12.48%	22.48%
L2040	(.096%)	13.89%	25.19%
L2050	(3.81%)		
L Income	2.33%	5.74%	8.57%

Transfers of TSP Death Benefits to "Inherited" IRAs

Non-spouse TSP beneficiaries can take advantage of a tax minimization strategy previously only available to spouse beneficiaries. They can now transfer their death benefit payments to an "inherited" IRA and, in most cases, take required payments from the IRA based on their own life expectancy. This eliminates the tax hit that many non-spouse beneficiaries were subject to before the law was changed. The rules governing inherited IRAs are complicated, and there are restrictions. You may wish to discuss this with your tax advisor.

Wider Opportunities for Transferring Tax-Exempt Money

Members of the uniformed services who contribute tax-exempt money to the TSP can now transfer it into a 403(b) annuity, if the 403(b) administrator accepts tax-exempt money.

Now separated TSP participants taking age-based withdrawals are able to transfer money directly from their TSP accounts to Roth IRAs. However, in the beginning, transfers to IRAs will not be available to participants who have an average gross income of $100,000 or more, or to participants who are married but filing separate tax returns. More information about this opportunity will be available once the IRS issues regulations.

Inter-Fund Transfers

You can make an inter-fund transfer in any month you wish, without an annual limit. You can transfer or shift any portion of money already in your account to any of the funds available. The most efficient way to request an inter-fund transfer is online (tsp.gov) or by using the ThriftLine, 504-255-8777.

Vesting in the TSP

Vesting is acquiring ownership of the money you put into your Thrift Savings Plan account. Once you are vested, all the money in the account belongs to you and can be taken out of the plan if you leave federal service. All employees are 100 percent vested in their own contributions and the earnings on their account. You are vested in the matching funds after three years of employment.

Loans from the TSP

A TSP loan program is available. You can borrow what you have contributed and the earnings on those contributions for a variety of reasons. There are two types of loans. You can apply for a general purpose loan with a repayment period of one to five years, or you can apply for a residential loan for the purchase of a primary residence with a repayment period of one to 15 years.

No documentation is required for a general purpose loan, but you must submit documentation to support the amount of a residential loan request. If you are a FERS employee, you can borrow only your portion, not the government's portion. The interest rate is the prevailing rate of interest for the G Fund. In the last few years, with the G Fund interest rates lower, the cost of borrowing from the Thrift Savings Plan has been substantially better than borrowing from banks or credit unions.

With the new record-keeping system came changes to TSP loan policies. New rules allow re-amortization more than once and you may make partial repayments. In addition, loan information will be on your statement, which will be issued quarterly. The TSP will charge a one-time application fee of $50 for a new loan, and you must wait 60 days before applying for a new loan once the original is paid off.

What are my withdrawal options?

When you retire, you have several TSP withdrawal options:

- You can take your Thrift Savings Plan funds as an annuity. If you select this option, you are taxed only on the amount you receive each month in an annuity.
- Another option is taking your entire Thrift Savings Plan funds in a lump sum. You will pay ordinary income taxes on the entire amount.
- You can choose to receive your account balance in monthly payments and pay taxes only on the amounts received.
- New rules allow any combination of the above options for a retiree's full withdrawal. In addition, you may make a one-time partial withdrawal after separation, as long as you did not take an age-based, in-service withdrawal. Withdrawal elections begin after you select a full withdrawal choice.
- If you are eligible for retirement benefits, you can leave the money in the TSP after you leave federal service. You can continue to change investments, but you cannot add to the fund after you retire. You can leave the money in your account until April 1 of the calendar year after you turn 70. At that time, you will be required to receive a minimal distribution which will be based on your age and life expectancy.
- You can withdraw your TSP funds at retirement (either voluntary or involuntary). A 10 percent tax penalty for early withdrawal may apply if you separate or retire before the calendar year in which you reach age 55 and withdraw the funds before age 59 ½. You should refer to the Summary of the Thrift Savings Plan for Federal Employees (available upon request from your personnel office) for further information.
- You can elect, at the time you retire, to transfer your TSP funds into another recognized retirement system. This would be possible if you go to work for some other entity after federal retirement. Your personnel office can check with the TSP Service Office to determine if your new retirement system is a recognized system.
- Another option is to have your agency roll the funds into an IRA. By

doing this, you keep these funds tax deferred until as early as age 59 ½ or as late as age 70. If there are any questions concerning your withdrawal options, you should check with your personnel office.

Q&A

When and how can I withdraw funds from the TSP?

You can withdraw funds from your TSP account while still employed for two reasons: financial hardship and a one-time single payment (of all or part of your account) for employees over age 59, without withdrawal penalties.

Hardship withdrawals by employees under age 59 are subject to early withdrawal penalties. These withdrawals are referred to as "in-service withdrawals" and apply to both CSRS and FERS employees.

What are the procedures for post-service withdrawals?

All TSP participants who separate from federal service have the same withdrawal options, regardless of their eligibility for retirement benefits. When you separate you become eligible to withdraw your TSP account. You have many options from which to choose, so carefully examine the packet of TSP information you will receive at retirement. Here are some examples:

- You may choose a TSP life annuity, a single payment, or a series of monthly payments.
- You may also leave your account in the TSP when you separate, and make a withdrawal later on.
- You may transfer part or all of your TSP funds to an IRA or other eligible (private industry) retirement plan, but if you choose an IRA or other eligible plan you cannot change your request.
- Also, you may have your payments begin immediately or at a later date, but not beyond your minimum required distribution age of 70.

These options are sometimes called "mix and match" withdrawals. Under the new regulations, you have a greater choice than was previously available.

How does the cost of health insurance change when I retire?

The cost of health insurance does not change when you retire. You pay the same as when you were an employee. The federal government pays the same. The basic difference is that you pay the premium on a monthly basis, usually out of your annuity check.

If both my spouse and I are federal employees, is it necessary for either or both of us to elect a survivor benefit to ensure that the surviving spouse will have health insurance?

No, neither of you will be required to elect a survivor benefit as long as you were both covered by federal health insurance at retirement and you submit an SF2809 for verification of your coverage.

I started at age 22. Can I leave at age 52?

FERS requires age 62 and five years of service; age 60 and 20 years of service; or "minimum retirement age" and 30 years of service. Your minimum retirement age is based on the year of your birth. FERS employees can also retire at the MRA and 10 years of service (benefits are reduced by 5 percent for your years under age 62).

So the quick answer is "no" and "maybe" for FERS employees if the specific requirements are met.

Can I count sick leave?

Sick leave counts in the computation of your annuity after you have met all the eligibility requirements for an immediate annuity. FERS employees receive 50 percent of accrued sick leave until December 31, 2013. Beginning in 2014, all sick leave counts.

Does locational pay count toward retirement?

Locality pay counts toward your high-3 salary and is used in the formula that determines your retirement pay.

If my spouse dies before I do, what happens to the cost/survivor benefits?

The reduction for survivor benefits stops and your annuity increases. The money you have paid for the spousal survivorship is not refunded to you.

Does my ex-spouse have rights?

Ex-spouses have certain rights under the provisions of the Spouse Equity Act. For example, a court may award a survivor annuity and/or TSP benefits to a former spouse.

If my disabled child receives a Social Security benefit does it affect my benefits?

A disabled child receiving Social Security benefits would not affect benefits you would receive.

Can I leave a benefit to a child?

Children are provided death benefits if they are under 18 and unmarried. An annually adjusted amount is determined by the number of children. Benefits may continue until age 22, if the child is in school. For FERS employees/annuitants, the child's benefits are reduced by any Social Security benefits the child receives. Benefits to children are provided without cost to the employee/annuitant.

What am I entitled to if I quit?

If you have retirement eligibility you could draw a pension, you could leave your money in the retirement system and draw a deferred retirement annuity at age 62, or you could withdraw all your retirement funds.

When should I retire?

You should retire when you are eligible and want to retire. There is no magic formula that makes the decision for you.

When will my annuity begin and will it be taxed?

If you are CSRS your annuity begins the next day — if you retire the last day of the month or the first, second, or third day of the month you become eligible. If you are FERS, your annuity begins the next day if you are eligible to retire on the last day of the month. Absolutely, your annuity will be taxed from Day One!

Are there differences between how states tax an annuity?

Every state is different in how it taxes annuities and some do not tax an annuity at all. Alaska, Florida, Nevada, New Hampshire, South Dakota, Tennessee, Texas, Washington, and Wyoming have no personal income taxes. Alabama, Hawaii, Illinois, Kansas, Louisiana, Massachusetts, Michigan, New York, and Pennsylvania exempt the total amount of a civil service annuity from taxation. In Kentucky, North Carolina, Oregon, and Wisconsin varying amounts of an annuity are exempt. Check with your state for specific laws.

If I postpone retirement, what happens to my health insurance?

Nothing. If you postpone retirement you pay just as you do now. Your health insurance premiums do not change in retirement.

How might Medicare Plus (state) affect my benefits/my Medicare?

It would not affect your retirement benefits or your entitlement to Medicare.

How will I know that my application for retirement is being processed?

Upon receipt of your retirement application from your personnel and payroll office, OPM will notify you that your application is being processed. They will provide you with a civil service claim identification number (e.g., CSA0000000). This number is required whenever you, or anyone on your behalf, contacts OPM concerning your annuity.

Who should I contact if I have questions before I receive a CSA number?

It normally takes about 30-45 days for OPM to issue a CSA number. If you need to check on the status of your application, you should contact your former payroll office to determine when your records were sent to OPM. Your payroll office should provide you with the number and date of the Register of Separations and Transfer. You will also need your payroll identification number.

Can I receive payments before my claim is processed?

As soon as OPM receives all of your records, they will begin making "interim payments." These interim payments normally begin within one to three months after the date of retirement. Interim payments can only be authorized if your records clearly show that you are eligible for retirement.

How much will my interim payment be?

Interim payments average approximately 85 percent of your projected final benefit. However, they may be less if:

1. You have received a refund for retirement deductions previously paid,
2. You have service after Oct. 1, 1982, not covered by the retirement system, or
3. You have service for which you have not made a deposit or redeposit.

Interim payments are subject to federal withholding tax. No premiums for health or life insurance will be withheld until you are placed in permanent pay status.

When are my checks due?

Monthly checks are due the first business day of the month.

When will I be placed in permanent payment status?

The majority of retirees are placed in permanent payment status within the first four months after retirement. At the time you are placed in permanent payment status, you will receive a refund of the amount withheld from your interim payments minus the premiums for health and life insurance.

What are my spouses Thrift Plan options when I die?
Spouses of deceased federal workers or military personnel enrolled in the Thrift Plan now have their own personal beneficiary participant accounts under their own names. Beneficiary participants accounts are automatically invested in the G fund, but users can make fund transfers into any TSP investment option.

CHAPTER 9

Personal Data Organizer

What records are necessary to keep?
Where should this information be kept?
Is one copy enough?

This is your personal planning portfolio. It provides you and your planning partner with a quick and easy reference for recording information about your key documents. It is designed to allow you to arrange data on all your records simply and concisely.

Record all information as completely as possible. In the event of an emergency or death, this information can be extremely important. Having everything organized means those who must make decisions will have the necessary information.

When you are finished with your personal inventory, place it in a safe location known to at least two other family members or close friends. Don't place the information in a safe deposit box because of limited access to it in time of need.

Finally, try to update this personal planning inventory with your planning partner once a year. Your time will be well spent.

Personal Data

Name (Maiden Name) _____

Date and place of birth _____

Birth certificate _____

Social Security # _____

Partner's Name _____

Date and place of birth _____

Birth certificate _____

Social Security # _____

Location of

Citizenship papers _____

Marriage certificate _____

Military papers DD-214 _____

_____

Divorce papers _____

State of jurisdiction _____

Parents

Father's Name _____

Date / place of birth _____

Date / place of death _____

Mother's Name _____

Date / place of birth _____

Date / place of death _____

Father's Name _____

Date and place of birth _____

Date and place of death _____

Mother's Name _____

Date and place of birth _____

Date and place of death _____

Children

NAME

TELEPHONE

ADDRESS

CITY/STATE/ZIP

NAME

TELEPHONE

ADDRESS

CITY/STATE/ZIP

NAME

TELEPHONE

ADDRESS

CITY/STATE/ZIP

NAME

TELEPHONE

ADDRESS

CITY/STATE/ZIP

NAME

TELEPHONE

ADDRESS

CITY/STATE/ZIP

NAME

TELEPHONE

ADDRESS

CITY/STATE/ZIP

Financial Records: Bank/Credit Union Accounts

❑ Checking ❑ Savings

_____
                              ACCOUNT NUMBER

_____
INSTITUTION   TELEPHONE

_____
ADDRESS

_____

❑ Checking ❑ Savings

_____
                              ACCOUNT NUMBER

_____
INSTITUTION   TELEPHONE

_____
ADDRESS

_____

❑ Checking ❑ Savings

_____
                              ACCOUNT NUMBER

_____
INSTITUTION   TELEPHONE

_____
ADDRESS

_____

❑ Checking ❑ Savings

_____
                              ACCOUNT NUMBER

_____
INSTITUTION   TELEPHONE

_____
ADDRESS

_____

Equity Funds

Document	Location	Identifying Number

Bond Funds

Document	Location	Identifying Number

Individual Stock

Document	Location	Identifying Number

REITs

Document	Location	Identifying Number

Cash & Cash Equivalents

Document	Location	Identifying Number

Personal Creditors or Debtors

Document	Amount	Identifying Number

Tax Records

Location of personal income tax returns/support information

Safe Deposit Box

COMPANY

ADDRESS

TELEPHONE   BOX NUMBER

LOCATION OF KEY

CONTENTS

Wills

LOCATION OF WILL

LOCATION OF COPY #2

DATE OF WILL

LAWYER   TELEPHONE

EXECUTOR   TELEPHONE

Property Records: Automobiles

TITLE LOCATION #1

BILL OF SALE

TAG RECEIPTS

TITLE LOCATION #2

BILL OF SALE

TAG RECEIPTS

Property Records: Real Estate

ADDRESS #1

TYPE OF PROPERTY

TITLE REGISTERED TO

TITLE INSURED BY

INSURER ADDRESS

INSURER TELEPHONE

MORTGAGE HOLDER

MORTGAGE HOLDER ADDRESS

MORTGAGE HOLDER TELEPHONE

LOCATION OF DEED/MORTGAGE

IS MORTGAGE PAID IN FULL?

LOCATION OF RECEIPTS

LOCATION OF TAX RECEIPTS

ADDRESS #2

TYPE OF PROPERTY

TITLE REGISTERED TO

TITLE INSURED BY

INSURER ADDRESS

INSURER TELEPHONE

MORTGAGE HOLDER

MORTGAGE HOLDER ADDRESS

MORTGAGE HOLDER TELEPHONE

LOCATION OF DEED/MORTGAGE

IS MORTGAGE PAID IN FULL?

LOCATION OF RECEIPTS

LOCATION OF TAX RECEIPTS

Personal Property

Jewelry, Fine Art, Antiques, Furniture, Boats, Coins, Family Items, Etc.

ITEM	LOCATION	INSURED?/AMOUNT

Insurance: Life Insurance

GROUP POLICY NUMBER   POLICY AMOUNT

POLICY LOCATION

OTHER POLICIES

Insurance: Medical Insurance

CARRIER

ADDRESS

POLICY NUMBER   POLICY AMOUNT   ID NUMBER

OTHER MEDICAL INSURANCE POLICIES

Insurance: Property Insurance

COMPANY NAME

AGENT   TELEPHONE

ADDRESS

POLICY NUMBER   POLICY AMOUNT

POLICY LOCATION

Insurance: Auto Insurance

COMPANY NAME

AGENT

ADDRESS

TELEPHONE   POLICY NUMBER   POLICY LOCATION

OTHER POLICIES

Employment History

PRESENT EMPLOYER

ADDRESS

TELEPHONE   YEARS

BENEFITS DUE:

SPOUSE'S EMPLOYER

ADDRESS

TELEPHONE   YEARS

BENEFITS DUE:

IRA, 401k, Roth, Deferred Savings, etc.

COMPANY

CONTACT

PHONE

COMPANY

CONTACT

PHONE

COMPANY

CONTACT

PHONE

COMPANY

CONTACT

PHONE

COMPANY

CONTACT

PHONE

Advisors

NAME   TELEPHONE

ADDRESS

Attorney

NAME   TELEPHONE

ADDRESS

Doctor

NAME   TELEPHONE

ADDRESS

Accountant

NAME   TELEPHONE

ADDRESS

Insurance Agent

NAME   TELEPHONE

ADDRESS

Banks/Banker

NAME   TELEPHONE

ADDRESS

Broker

NAME   TELEPHONE

ADDRESS

Executor

NAME   TELEPHONE

ADDRESS

Clergy

NAME   TELEPHONE

ADDRESS

Resources

Financial Planning

Bonds, buying bonds on line (**savingsbonds.gov**).

Bureau of the Public Debt (**pubdebt.treas.gov**). Find information about U.S. savings bonds, Treasury bills and bonds. Learn of upcoming Treasury auctions or link to the Federal Reserve Board of New York's online savings-bond-redemption-value calculator. (Also treasury.gov).

CardTrack (cardtrak.com) Search and compare credit cards and card offers. Provides monthly comparative credit card tables as published in the Wall Street Journal.

Certified Financial Planner Board of Standards (**cfp-board.org**). Useful consumer section.

CNNfn (**cnnfn.com**) CNN Financial. Find investing ideas and analysis.

College answers (**collegeanswer.com**). Get side-by-side comparisons of college costs.

College Savings Plans Network (collegesavings.org) Cost calculators, information and a comparison tool for state and private 529 college savings plans.

College XPress (**collegexpress.com**). Planning, admission, application, school profiles.

Credit reports (**experian.com, tuc.com/, equifax.com**).

Credit score information (**fairisaac.com**).

Dalbar and Microsoft (**moneycentral.msn.com/investor/dalbar**). Find planners in your area. Enter the size of your portfolio, the type of planning you need, and your preferences in a planner. Advisors have at least five years of experience, a clean record with financial regulators, and a background in the specialty you request.

Financenter (financeneter.com) Financial calculators for many situations concerning your home, car and credit cards.

Financial Aid Information Page (**finaid.org**). Connect with college financial-aid offices, link to a database of scholarships and lists of student-aid lenders.

Financial Planning Association (**fpanet.org**), 3801 E. Florida Ave., Suite 708, Denver, CO 80210-2544; 800-322-4237.

Garrett Planning Network (**garrettplanningnetwork.com**). A group of advisers who charge by the hour.

Health Insurance Association of America (ahip.org) Information and resources regarding insurance products.

Insurance News Network (**insure.com**). Get rules and rates for about 20 states on choosing auto, home, and life insurance.

Insurance quotes (**directquote.com**), (**bestquote.com**).

Internal Revenue Service (**irs.gov**). Find tax information for individuals and businesses. Search tax regulations and download forms and publications.

INVESTools (investools.**com**). Reference financial newsletters and publications by typing the name or symbol of the company; references are displayed, along with hypertext links and cost.

Life (**lifehappens.org**). Find a glossary of insurance terms and an online calculator that figures life and disability insurance needs.

Morningstar (**morningstar.com**). Get updates from this mutual fund rating firm.

Mortgage rates (**americanloansearch.com**), (**bankrate.com**).

National Association of Personal Financial Advisors (**napfa.org**); 847-483-5400.

National Endowment for Financial Education (nefe.org) Tools and information to manage money wisely and to turn their financial education into action.

National Foundation for Consumer Credit (**nfcc.org**), 8611 Second Ave., Suite 100, Silver Spring, MD 20910; 301-589-5600; fax: 301-495-5623; office locator 800-388-2227.

Office of Thrift Supervision (**ots.treas.gov**). Savings bank information.

Quicken Insure Market (**insweb.com**). Get instant price quotes on life insurance and nearest agents. Auto insurance quotes are also available.

Roth IRA (RothIRA.com) Calculators and information for Roth IRAs contributions and savings, including conversion calculators.

SavingForCollege.com Variety of tools and calculators to help you with creating a plan to save for college expenses.

Stocks (**netstockdirect.com**). Buy stocks direct from companies.

U.S. Treasury (**ustreas.gov**). Fund value of savings and bonds.

Financial Apps

Betterment (betterment.com). Uses a risk dial to allocate your portfolio as simply as possible.

HelloWallet (hellowallet.com). Tracks users' locations to tell them how a purchase will affect their budgets.

Mint (mint.com). Collects financial data in one place.

Pageonce (pageonce.com). Charges fees for a mobile bill-payment service.

Personal Capital (personalcapital.com). Combines automated financial analysis with real-life financial planners.

SigFig (sigfig.com) Aggregates your investment accounts and analyzes their cost and allocations.

Stickk.com (stick.com). Offers to penalize users who fall short of their goals.

Yodlee Money Center (moneycenter.yodlee.com). Aggregates your accounts and shows a complete financial picture.

Legal Issues

American Bar Association (**abanet.org**), 750 N. Lakeshore Dr., Chicago, IL 60611-4403; 312-988-5000.

Legal advice (**freeadvice.com**), (**lawguru.com**).

Nolo Press Self-Help Law Center (**nolo.com**). Find self-help articles on taxes, mediation, estate planning, homeowners, landlords/tenants, etc.

Health and Wellness

American Medical Association's Physician Select (**dbapps.ama-assn.org**). Online assistance in finding a doctor.

Centers for Disease Control and Prevention (**cdc.gov**).

Evaluate doctors (**healthmarket.com**).

National Institutes of Health (**nih.gov**).

WebMD Physician Directory (**My.webmd.com**). Online directory of physicians and "quick reference of information about physicians."

Family Issues

American Association of Retired Persons (**aarp.org**) offers details on types of help available.

College funding (**finaid.com**), (**collegesavings.org**).

College information (**collegeboard.org**).

Eldercare Locator (**eldercare.gov**), 927 115th St. NW, 6th floor, Washington, DC 20005; 800-677-1116. Identifies state and local agencies on aging that can refer you to local services by zip code area.

Eldercare Web (**elderweb.com**). Find resources for the elderly and their caregivers. State-specific information is included.

Elderhostel (**elderhostel.org**), 75 Federal St., Boston, MA 02110-1941; 877-426-8056.

Geriatric Care Managers (**caremanager.org**), 1604 N. Country Club Rd., Tucson, AZ 85716; 520-881-8008.

National Association for Home Care (**nahc.org**), 202-547-7424, offers *How to Choose a Home Care Provider: a Consumer Guide*. Write to 228 7th St. SE, Washington, D.C. 20003.

National Family Caregivers Association (**nfcacares.org**), 800-896-3650, offers support and information.

Nursing home comparisons (**medicare.gov**).

Senior day care etc. (**careguide.com**), National Association for Home Care, (**nahc.org**).

U.S. Administration on Aging (**aoa.gov**) offers details on local resources and links to other useful web sites.

Visiting Nurse Association of America (**vnaa.org**) can identify local visiting nurse agencies that operate in 40 states; 888-866-8773.

Career Planning

CareerMosaic (**careermosaic.com**). Use the Career Resource Center to learn to write a resume; research job trends, industries and companies. Find job listings (including international opportunities) and links to employers' home pages.

Futurestep (**futurestep.com**). Highly competitive online recruitment site with limited (12,000) listings.

Management Recruiters International (**mrinetwork.com**). Helps you find the right recruiter or customize a job search.

The Monster Board (**monster.com**). Search for jobs by location, discipline or company and post an online resume. Free access to more than 350 companies with job listings.

Social Security

Social Security Online (**ssa.gov**). Request an estimate of future benefits, apply for a new or replacement card, or get information on benefits programs. You can also check COLAs and current earnings limitations. 800-772-1213.

Tax Planning

American Institute of Certified Public Accountants (**aicpa.org**), Harborside Financial Center, 201 Plaza 3, Jersey City, NJ 07311-3881; 888-777-7077.

NannyTax (**nannytax.com**). Get information on employment taxes, both federal and state, when you hire household help.

Index